Britain
IN THE EUROPEAN UNION

CW00497408

Britain

IN THE EUROPEAN UNION

Second edition

Andrew Geddes

First published 1999 by
Baseline Book Company
PO Box 8
Tisbury
Wiltshire SP3 6QY

British Library Cataloguing
ISBN 1 897626 14 2

Designed by Price Watkins
Printed and bound by Galliards, Great Yarmouth

Acknowledgements

I am grateful to Valérie Amiraux, Christopher Hill and Magnus Ryner for their
help with sections of this book. Responsibility for the final version is of course
mine alone.

Contents

Tables

Abbreviations

ASEAN	Association of South East Asian Nations
CAP	common agricultural policy
CFSP	common foreign and security policy
COPA	Committee of Agricultural Organisations
COREPER	Committee of Permanent Representatives
DM	Deutschmark
DUP	Democratic Unionist Party (Northern Ireland)
EAGGF	European Agricultural Guidance and Guarantee Fund
EC	European Community
ECHR	European Convention on Human Rights
ECJ	European Court of Justice
ECOFIN	Economics and Finance Ministers' Council
ECSC	European Coal and Steel Community
Ecu	European Currency Unit
EDC	European Defence Community
EEA	European Economic Area
EEC	European Economic Community
EFTA	European Free Trade Area
EMS	European Monetary System
EMU	economic and monetary union
EPC	European Political Cooperation
EPP	European People's Party
ERDF	European Regional Development Fund
ERM	exchange rate mechanism
ESF	European Social Fund
ETUC	European Trades Union Congress
EU	European Union
EUF	European Union of Federalists
Euratom	European Atomic Energy Community
FRG	Federal Republic of Germany
GATT	General Agreement on Tariffs and Trade
GDP	gross domestic product
GDR	German Democratic Republic
GNP	gross national product
IGC	intergovernmental conference
JHA	Justice and Home Affairs Policy
MAFF	Ministry of Agriculture, Fisheries and Food
NAFTA	North American Free-Trade Agreement
NATO	North Atlantic Treaty Organisation
NFU	National Farmers' Union
NWRA	North West Regional Assocation
OEEC	Organisation for European Economic Cooperation

OUP	Ulster ('Official') Unionist Party (Northern Ireland)
PR	proportional representation
QMV	qualified majority voting
SDLP	Social Democratic and Labour Party (Northern Ireland)
SDP	Social Democratic Party
SEA	Single European Act
SNP	Scottish National Party
TUC	Trades Union Congress
TUPE	Transfer of Undertakings (Protection of Employment)
UKIP	UK Independence Party
UKREP	UK Permanent Representation of the EC
UNICE	Union of Industries of the EC
UUP	Ulster Unionist Party
VAT	value added tax
WEU	West European Union

Introduction

The European Union (EU) casts an increasingly long shadow over many of the key issues in contemporary British politics. Britain's economy is closely tied to those of other EU member states while hot-tempered disputes over European integration and the divisions they caused were central to the electoral obliteration of the Conservative Party at the 1997 general election. Yet even though politicians and newspapers seemed obsessed with the European issue and its implications for, among other things, national sovereignty, the British people remained distinctly underwhelmed and were far less interested in the EU than the political élites. As the Eurosceptical *Daily Express* noted in the run-up to the 1997 general election, 'it's the issue that makes the parties swoon and the voters yawn'. One reason for this is that the EU can still seem remote from people's day-to-day concerns about employment, health care, education and the like. A key implication of European integration is that domestic and European politics are actually becoming increasingly entwined, as this book shows. The effect of this is that a European dimension is being imparted to key economic and political issues. It is imperative to have some understanding of the Union's history, institutions and policies and venture into what some see as the impenetrable maze of EU politics, but which in reality is no more (and perhaps less) complicated than political systems in member states. The key point about the EU is that it is supranational. This means that in certain areas, such as trade and agriculture, its member states have ceded power, or sovereignty, to Union-level institutions to make decisions which are legally binding on them. This supranationalism is both a central and a controversial aspect of the EU. Its implications for Britain are the focus of this book.

What are we talking about? One puzzling aspect of analysing European integration is the plethora of terms used to describe it: the EU, the European Economic Community (EEC), the European Community (EC), the Common Market, the Union, the Community, to name six. It may be even more puzzling that all basically refer to the same organisation. The key point is that the Maastricht Treaty (1992) created the European Union and since the Treaty was finally ratified in November 1993 it has become usual to see references to the EU. This is the term most frequently employed throughout this book. At various points, however, readers are likely to encounter others terms or acronyms such as the Common Market, the EEC or EC. All these terms have historical, legal or political importance. To highlight their significance and explain the development of European integration, terms other than the EU will be used when appropriate. These situations will be clearly explained and the relation between these terms and acronyms and what we now know as the EU will become evident. When analysing events before the Maastricht Treaty created the EU, it is accurate to refer to the EEC, EC or Community, as will often be done in the book's early chapters.

Britain in the European Union

Britain distrusted the supranational aspirations of the nascent European Community in the 1950s and 1960s and since it joined the EC on 1 January 1973 has acquired the reputation of being a reluctant European. Whether this is justified can only be determined by looking both at the development of British policy towards the EU and at how EU membership has affected Britain.

Membership of the EU has had an extensive impact on the British economy, politics and society. Responsibility for important policy sectors has been transferred to EU institutions. Decisions made by EU institutions can override national law. As power has been ceded to the Union so political activity has been refocused. Government ministers frequently meet with colleagues from other member states in EU decision-making forums. Some pressure groups now look to Brussels as much as to Whitehall. Consequently, it is important to understand the workings of EU institutions and not to regard the EU simply as a 'foreign policy' issue. Its remit stretches to a wide range of domestic activities.

Although Britain is now deeply involved in the EU, it is important not to exaggerate its centrality to the Union. Britain, for a variety of reasons, has always been peripheral to the economic and political integration which has characterised EU history. Having been the leading European nation at the end of the Second World War, Britain became marginalised from the development of the EU. In 1997, after 18 years of Conservative government during which relations with other EU member states and Union institutions had at times been acrimonious, Tony Blair pledged a more constructive approach to the EU. His predecessor, John Major, had made similar remarks when he took over from Margaret Thatcher. Blair pledged to 'modernise' the EU in the same way that he planned to effect similar changes in the UK. The substantive components of this modernisation agenda can appear unclear. Moreover, the receptiveness of heads of government from other EU member states to British proposals for modernisation must be viewed with some caution because of Britain's reputation for awkwardness. Other member states may be reluctant to accept lessons from the UK on future development of the Union, particularly when Britain is still 'waiting and seeing' about the EU's central objective, the creation of a single currency within an economic and monetary union.

EU facts and figures   The EU is an economic and a political entity, and seeks integration at both levels. The precise link between these two processes is, however, a matter of great contention. Some argue that economic integration should be separated from political. Others maintain that no such separation is possible. Underlying this debate is an undeniable drive towards economic integration in Europe accompanied by the development of a political-institutional framework to back up economic objectives. All statistics show that the EU is increasingly becoming a single economic area. The EU has also assumed an increased role in pursuit of what is called 'economic and social cohesion', which takes in policy areas like regional development and aspects of social policy. Moreover, since 1993 all citizens of member states have been citizens of the Union.

There are currently 15 members of the EU. Its founders were France, West Germany, Italy, Belgium, the Netherlands and Luxembourg. In 1951 these six countries signed the Treaty of Paris which established the European Coal and Steel Community (ECSC). In 1957 they signed the Treaties of Rome which created the European Economic Community (EEC) – or Common Market – and the European Atomic Energy Community (Euratom).

In 1973 Britain, Ireland and Denmark joined, to be followed in 1981 by Greece and in 1986 by Portugal and Spain. The Maastricht Treaty, signed in February 1992 and finally ratified in November 1993, created a European Union with citizens of the 12 member states becoming citizens of the Union. In 1995 membership expanded to 15 when Austria, Finland and Sweden joined. The Norwegians rejected membership in a referendum, just as they had done in 1972. In 1996 and 1997 the functioning of the Union was reviewed with the resultant Amsterdam Treaty (negotiated in June 1997, signed in October, but at time of writing not ratified in all member states) intended as the equivalent of a 5000-mile service on policies and institutions. Amsterdam's centrepiece was the creation of 'an area of freedom, justice and security' within which citizens of EU member states would be able to move freely. The EU would assume responsibility for aspects of immigration and asylum policy. Britain opted out of these provisions because it wanted to maintain its own border controls. Amsterdam was also supposed to lay the foundations for EU enlargement, although it fudged many key questions about the future role of EU institutions. Central, eastern and southern European countries are queueing up for membership. Membership of the Union could increase to about 25 countries by early in the twenty-first century.

Total EU population in 1997 was just over 370 million (Table 0.1), the largest member country being the reunified Germany created in 1991 following the collapse of the German Democratic Republic (GDR). For comparison, the USA has a population of 260 million, and Japan a population of 125 million.

Table 0.1 | **Population of the European Union, 1997**

Austria	8,068,000
Belgium	10,170,000
Denmark	5,275,000
Finland	5,132,000
France	58,492,000
Germany	82,012,000
Greece	10,487,000
Ireland	3,652,000
Italy	57,461,000
Luxembourg	418,000
Netherlands	15,567,000
Portugal	9,934,000
Spain	39,299,000
Sweden	8,844,000
UK	58,902,000
EU15	373,713,000

Source Eurostat

A salient characteristic of the EU is intensification throughout its history of trading links between member states (Table 0.2). In 1958 Britain exported just over one-fifth of its products to the countries which were later to be its EU partners. By 1994 this proportion had increased to more than half. The pattern of imports from EU countries developed in pretty similar fashion over the same period. Britain does, though, still maintain significant trade links with non-EU countries, particularly the USA and Japan. Indeed, Britain is by far the biggest foreign investor in non-EU member states and the biggest European recipient of foreign investment. This means that Britan is far more integrated into the global economy than other EU member states. That said, 54 per cent of the UK's combined imports and exports in 1997 were with other EU member states; although this compares with an EU average of about two thirds.

Table 0.2 | **Intensification of intra-EU trade, 1958-94**

	% exports to other member states		% imports from other member states	
	1958	1994	1958	1994
Belgium/Lux	55.4	72.1	55.1	68.1
Denmark	59.3	52.3	60.0	52.1
Germany	37.9	48.9	36.3	50.7
Greece	50.9	54.2	53.7	64.4
France	30.9	60.7	28.3	65.0
Ireland	82.4	70.0	68.9	63.3
Italy	34.5	53.4	30.2	56.2
Netherlands	58.3	74.7	50.7	54.8
Portugal	38.9	75.1	53.4	71.4
Spain	46.8	64.5	31.8	63.5
UK	21.7	54.1	21.8	49.9
EU12	37.2	58.4	35.2	57.0

Source 'European Economy' 1997

The web of interdependence created by ever stronger trading links means that the economic health of individual member states depends increasingly on the prosperity of their Union partners. Consequently prosperity becomes a collective endeavour. However, the strengthening of trading links within the EU has not helped overcome the cyclical nature of capitalist economic development. EU economies entered recession in the early 1990s and unemployment reached very high levels (Table 0.3).

Table 0.3 | **EU unemployment, March 1998 (%)**

Austria	4.5
Belgium	9.0
Denmark	4.8
France	12.0
Germany	10.0
Greece*	9.6
Ireland	9.4
Italy**	12.0
Luxembourg	2.2
Netherlands***	4.6
Portugal	6.5
Spain***	19.5
Sweden	8.3
UK***	6.5
EU 15	10.3

*1997; **January 1998; ***February 1998

Source Eurostat

Unfortunately for Britain it joined the EC in 1973 at the very moment when EC economies entered the recession that followed the increase in oil prices and when the integrative process moved into a period of stagnation. This raised doubts, not least in Britain, about the benefits of membership. Recession in the early 1990s prompted similar doubts. As the European Union becomes central to member state economies so economic problems tend to be laid at the door of the Union. Support for integration dwindles during hard times.

Yet there is no doubt that EU membership has been linked in the past with high growth rates. Whether there is a relationship of cause and effect here is disputable. Table 0.4 shows GDP per capita 1970-97 for EU members. The relative economic decline of Britain is striking. By this measure, the UK was the twelfth-richest EU member state by 1997. Relative decline began before Britain gained membership of the Community, and has not been arrested since.

Table 0.4 | **GDP per capita in EU member states, 1970-97**[1]

	1970	1980	1990	1997
Belgium	113.0	120.8	102.7	111.4
Denmark	137.4	129.4	132.7	144.6
Germany	130.2	131.5	125.3	123.4
Greece	58.7	50.2	43.4	51.8
Spain	47.7	56.5	66.9	64.9
France	120.5	123.3	111.3	113.2
Ireland	59.5	59.7	68.7	89.5
Italy	85.4	79.7	101.8	92.5
Luxembourg	153.5	137.9	143.1	175.3
Netherlands	111.5	121.5	100.2	108.6
Austria	82.9	101.8	108.4	120.0
Portugal	34.9	29.4	36.1	47.7
Finland	101.2	107.5	142.8	107.2
Sweden	179.2	150.9	141.7	125.8
UK	95.3	95.2	89.7	86.9

1 Calculated at current market prices; EU=100

Source 'European Economy'

Relatively high economic growth has made the EU one of the most powerful economic blocs in the world, and one of the most important markets. These are major reasons for expansion of the Union since the 1970s and for the current queue of applicants. Yet the gains of membership secured by Britain remain unclear and are difficult to disentangle from relative economic and political decline.

British membership assessed

The central aim of this book is to assess British membership of the EU, which has now lasted for more than 25 years. It begins by introducing the terminology of European integration. Chapter 1 explains many of the terms used by analysts of European integration – including supranationalism, intergovernmentalism, sovereignty and federalism – and looks at ways in which the use of such terminology can inform an assessment of Britain's EU membership.

Chapter 2 focuses on the historical origins of European integration and the emergence of the ECSC, Euratom and the EEC in the 1950s. It also examines the failure to create a European Defence Community in 1954. Chapter 3 appraises the policy of successive British governments towards the Community. It asks why Britain did not join the Community in the 1950s and why Britain then decided to seek entry in the 1960s. The policies of successive British governments since accession in 1973, from Edward Heath's to Tony Blair's, are then appraised.

Chapter 4 analyses the institutional structure of the European Union. It looks at the power and responsibilities of the Commission, the Council of Ministers, the European Parliament, the Court of Justice and the European Council. It also asks whether there is a 'democratic deficit' in the EU. The Maastricht and Amsterdam Treaties are the focus of Chapter 5. Are these treaties the blueprints for a federal Europe? Maastricht contained proposals for economic and monetary union, social policy, foreign and security policy and interior policy that aroused controversy across the Union. The 1997 Amsterdam Treaty was less ambitious and attracted less attention, but has far-reaching significance through its creation of an area of 'freedom, justice and security' where the EU assumes more responsibility for free movement of people, immigration and asylum policy, from which Britain opted out.

Chapter 6 examines the policy responsibilities of the Union. It looks at principal areas of activity such as agriculture and regional aid, and also assesses some of the more day-to-day implications of Community membership for people in Britain. Chapter 7 surveys the likelihood of new members from central, eastern and southern Europe entering the Union early in the twenty-first century, and also considers prospects for deeper integration. Is it possible to have a 'wider' Union with more members and 'deeper' economic and political integration? Chapter 8 looks at the myriad influences on British political and economic life of Union membership and asks how well integrated into the EU Britain has become. The Conclusion speculates on future development of the Union and Britain's role in it.

Debates about the EU and its integrative potential have a habit of generating more heat than light. The chapters that follow seek to illuminate some of the more salient features of an organisation that has become central to political and economic life in Britain.

1 Eurospeak

European integration provokes both fervent support and deep mistrust. Yet key terms used in debates about integration are often obscure or misunderstood. The first task is to acquire a basic understanding of the meaning such terms as integration, supranationalism, sovereignty and federalism. Later chapters will show that Britain's preference has always been for intergovernmentalism. Consequently, supranationalism has always been viewed with great wariness.

Integration

A conceptual framework – a way of thinking – about European integration is needed. Otherwise any analysis is no more than a collection of dates and facts within which assumptions about the nature of the integrative process remain implicit and obscured rather than explicit and explained. Indeed, the very meaning of Europe also needs to be made clear: 'there is no single or agreed Europe'.[1] The EC emerged during the Cold War and was composed of capitalist economies in western Europe. In the 1990s, following the collapse of the Soviet bloc, it faces the challenge of responding to the 'new Europe'. This immediately makes the point that the EU and Europe are not one and the same thing. The two terms cannot be transposed. Within the wider Europe a complex web of interdependent states and markets cooperate in an array of organisations. What is significant about the EU, and distinguishes it from other organisations, is that it is supranational. This term will itself be analysed later in this chapter.

Integration has been defined as 'a process for the creation of political communities' within which 'states cease to be wholly sovereign'.[2] In post-war Europe the main drive has been towards *economic integration*. Such integration can be divided into five main types:[3]

● A **free trade area** within which tariffs and quotas are eliminated between member countries
● A **customs union** within which tariffs and quotas are removed and an external tariff is imposed on goods and services entering the union
● A **single market** within which people, goods, services and capital can move freely
● An **economic and monetary union** involving a single currency and harmonisation of some national economic policies
● **Total economic integration** whereby the same economic policies are pursued in all the member states.

In the 1950s Britain preferred to limit itself to the first of these five levels of integration. In July 1959 it established the European Free Trade Area (EFTA) with six other countries (Austria, Denmark, Norway, Portugal, Sweden and Switzerland). Britain, like many of its EFTA partners, was fearful of the implications for national sovereignty of the EC, which was a customs union and had supranational structures. In subsequent years many of the EFTA countries nevertheless lodged applications to join. In 1986 the Single European Act set the EC on course for the third level of economic integration – a single market – within which people, goods, services and capital would move freely. The single European market officially came into being on 1 January 1993, though it has not yet been fully realised. In 1991 the Maastricht Treaty embodied plans for progress towards the fourth level – economic and monetary union – which is likely to be achieved early in the next century when it is planned that the European single currency, the euro, will go into circulation. On 1 January 1999, 11 EU member states established an economic and monetary union in the boldest instance of European integration since the signing of the Treaty of Rome in 1957.

Economic integration and the interdependence it generates may create pressure for political integration. There are four aspects to this:[4]

● **Institutional integration** comprising the growth of collective decision-making structures with common institutions and formal rules
● **Policy integration** whereby responsibility for particular policies is transferred to the supranational level
● **Attitudinal integration** which involves growth of support among the peoples of the participating countries
● **Security integration** whereby states expect non-violent relations.

There is clear evidence of institutional and policy integration in the EU with the development of common institutions such as the European Commission and the European Parliament and common policies such as the Common Agricultural Policy (CAP). Despite there being a high level of support for the general objectives of European integration, few will be unfamiliar with the events of 1992 and 1993 when the Maastricht Treaty staggered through its ratification process. The Danes rejected the Treaty in a referendum held in June 1992, when 51 per cent voted 'No' and 49 per cent 'Yes'. The people of France delivered no more than a *petit oui* to Maastricht in September 1992, when 51 per cent voted 'Yes' and 49 per cent 'No'.

Part of the problem is that the process of European integration tends to be driven by political and economic élites. Despite the founding

Treaties' aspiration to create 'a closer union of the peoples of Europe', EU institutions can seem distant from the people whose interests they are supposed to serve. There is talk of a 'democratic deficit' in the European Union, an absence of democracy and accountability which prevents it from acquiring the political legitimacy necessary to attitudinal integration.

When it comes to security integration it is important to note the strong Atlanticist tinge given to the defence of western Europe by the North Atlantic Treaty Organisation (NATO). America provided the security umbrella for the liberal democracies of western Europe during the Cold War. In these years Atlanticism, not Europeanism, shaped the collective defence structures of western Europe. Even now it remains an important aspect of EU thinking.

Supra-nationalism

Britain chose not to participate in the creation of the EC in the 1950s. One of the reasons for this was a deep distrust of the aspirations of the founder member states. Britain did not favour supranationalism because it feared the implications for national sovereignty. The EU is a good example of supranationalism, whereby formal structures of government are established above the nation state. There are three key features of supranational government:[5]

● The institutions of the supranational government are independent from those of member states
● The organisation can make rules that bind members and has the power to enforce those rules
● The institutions of the supranational government are part of a new legal system to which member states and individuals are subject.

EU law overrides national law, and institutions exist at the supranational (EU) level that are independent of member states. Supranational government has clear implications for national sovereignty. National sovereignty means that a country has supreme authority within its territory. Any country that is bound by the rules of a supranational organisation no longer has supreme authority, and is therefore no longer fully sovereign.

Britain has always preferred *intergovernmental cooperation* to supranational government. Intergovernmentalism implies unanimity as the basis of decision-making, and allows a veto to be exercised to protect national interests. However, the founders of the EC – France, Germany, Italy and the Benelux countries – were suspicious of political systems based on the notion of a national veto, and sought to move away from intergovernmentalism. They pointed to the intergovernmental League of Nations which, in the inter-war period, was for a number of reasons unable to exert the authority necessary to prevent drift towards the Second World War.

Sovereignty

A sovereign state holds and exercises supreme authority within its territorial jurisdiction. For many years, the United Kingdom of Great Britain and Northern Ireland was formally a sovereign state. However, any country which signs up to a supranational body of law, such as that which established the EU, is compromising its sovereignty because law which is determined collectively overrides that which it creates itself. EU law is binding on member states.

In Britain sovereign authority is vested in Parliament. The British constitution can be summed up in six words: what the monarch in Parliament decides. By joining the EC the British Parliament reduced its own sovereignty because in some areas supranational institutions such as the Council of Ministers and the Commission make laws.

Opponents of the EU argue that loss of sovereignty in a democratic political system reduces the rights of citizens to exercise control over decision-making authority. The ultimate recourse of the British electorate is to 'kick the rascals out' by voting for a change of government at a general election. However, if the national government is no longer the sovereign authority then national elections and policy preferences expressed in them may make little difference if they run counter to preferences agreed at Union level.

Advocates of European integration argue that sovereignty is not a static concept to be jealously guarded. Rather, it is to be utilised to benefit the citizens of a state. Membership of the EU means that sovereignty is 'pooled' at supranational level in some policy areas, such as trade, where it can be utilised more effectively. Put simply, 15 are stronger than one, and are far more likely to secure beneficial results for Union citizens than are the unilateral actions of one country.

Sovereignty, or as Margaret Thatcher put it 'who decides', has been central to Britain's relationship with the Community. There is, however, an important distinction to be made between *formal* and *informal* aspects of sovereignty:

> it has been the formal and visible transfer of sovereignty
> embodied in the issue of UK membership of the EC which has
> provided the main focus for public concern... Successive British
> governments have taken a pragmatic, even a relaxed attitude to

the informal processes of international interdependence, and the consequent erosion of national sovereignty.[6]

The point is that to focus on formal aspects of sovereignty, such as supposed parliamentary supremacy, may be to neglect disguised informal transfers of sovereignty that heighten Britain's inter-dependence within the international economic and political order. Formally, Britain was still a sovereign nation before it joined the EC in 1973. Yet informally it was losing sovereignty on an annual basis because economic integration in an increasingly interdependent world reduced its ability to control its own affairs.

Indeed, Ramsay MacDonald's Labour government had found itself largely at the mercy of international financiers in 1931, and Harold Wilson's Labour government had been similarly embarrassed in 1967 when devaluation of the pound was forced. Even in 1973, then, it could hardly be argued that Britain was in all senses a 'sovereign' nation. In years since then the point has been made ever more clearly. Ironically, Thatcher may have hastened processes of informal integration by relaxing exchange controls in 1979, thereby removing a potential power from the armoury of British government. Even when sterling 'floated' out of the Exchange Rate Mechanism (ERM) in September 1992 Britain found that its economic policy continued to be greatly influenced by decisions taken by the German Bundesbank. It is also worth noting that defence sovereignty has been 'pooled' for more than 50 years within NATO and beneath the umbrella of American protection.

The issues of supranationalism and sovereignty lead directly to what for some is the dreaded 'F-word': federalism.

Federalism

In earlier ages Britain, through plans drawn up for former colonies, was one of the world's great federalisers.[7] However, British governments have consistently seen federation as appropriate for others, not for the British. The British system of government is *unitary*: local government is subordinate to central. In Britain local government only exists because central government gives it tasks and responsibilities, and as it gives those tasks so it can take them away. The Labour government formed in May 1997 has devolved some powers to elected assemblies in Scotland, Wales and Northern Ireland, and has also raised the possibility of English regional government. This kind of regionalisation may produce a better fit between the UK system of government and the emergent EU system, which emphasises regional development.

In federal systems, such as the United States and Germany, neither the central nor the regional level of government is supposed to be subordinate to the other. Federalism is seen as generating effective central power for handling common problems while preserving regional autonomy. Five main features of a federal system of government can be highlighted:[8]

● Two levels of government, a general and a regional
● Formal distribution of legislative and executive authority and sources of revenue between the two levels
● A written constitution
● A supreme or constitutional court to adjudicate in disputes between the two levels
● Central institutions, including a bicameral legislature within which the upper chamber will usually embody territorial representation, as in the case with the US Senate and the German Bundesrat.

In the EU there are some signs of federation. Clearly there are two levels of government (in fact more because of regional and local government), each of which has its own budgetary resources. In addition, an established body of European law overrides national law. The European Court of Justice (ECJ) acts as umpire in disputes between supranational and national levels of government. Bulmer and Wessels argue that what is emerging is a system of 'cooperative federalism': the EU and national governments share responsibility for problem-solving because neither has the legal authority or policy competence to tackle the challenges that they face on their own.[9]

In Britain opponents of a 'federal Europe' use the term in a way markedly different from most federalists' understanding. For its opponents a 'federal Europe' means a European superstate with a huge centralised bureaucracy limiting the sovereign authority of member states. Advocates, on the other hand, see federation as a way of combining the political virtues of unity and diversity. For them, federalism is a means of decentralising power, not centralising it.

Subsidiarity

Resolution of the dispute between federalists and anti-federalists depends in large measure on questions of detail. The key is to decide which powers are to go to which level, supranational, national or subnational. In the late 1980s and the early 1990s the EU has been keen to proceed on the basis of what is known as *subsidiarity*, maintaining that power should be exercised at the lowest appropriate level. Subsidiarity is a rather amorphous notion and is one of the words used in debates on the European Union that baffles people as much as it informs them. In 1992 Commission President Jacques Delors offered a job and Ecu 200,000 to anyone who could define subsidiarity in one page.

The word originates from the Latin *subsidium*, meaning reserve troops. It first appeared in Pope Leo XIII's 1891 encyclical. In 1931 Pope Pius XI used it to denote that political and social decisions should not be taken at a higher level than necessary. The EU's leaders seized on this in the late 1980s, seeing it as a way of bridging the gap between the people and the Union. But lawyers warned of the dangers of taking a religious principle and converting it into a legal text.

British governments have tended to view subsidiarity as implying a division of responsibility between the EU and member states, with member states holding the upper hand. Subsidiarity could also mean powers going to lower levels of government. This could mean a transfer of power to regions or, in Britain, to Scotland, Wales and Northern Ireland. Germans tend to see subsidiarity as meaning a distribution of power between regions (*Länder*), Berlin and Brussels. Smaller member states, such as the Netherlands, Belgium and Luxembourg, have often blocked reduction in the powers of the Commission which they believe gives a voice to smaller member states. Since 1992 the Commission has been obliged to incorporate a subsidiarity justification in legislative proposals.

Regionalists seek a 'Europe of the regions' with nation states bypassed as powers move down to the local level and up to the EU.[10] The Commission has encouraged links between regions and the EU and between regions themselves, especially those that straddle borders. The European Parliament's 1988 Charter of the Regions is a further indication of the importance supranational institutions give to the fostering of regional identities within the Union. The Maastricht Treaty established an advisory Committee of the Regions which by 1998 comprised 222 representatives of local and regional authorities. It held its first plenary session in March 1994.

Neo-functionalism

If there are signs of federation in the EU, what forces are driving this process? Why has integration occurred? In the wake of the devastation wrought by the Second World War the European Union of Federalists (EUF) was established. Many of its members fought in the resistance against the Nazis. The EUF hoped that a United States of Europe could emerge to shape post-war Europe. For them maintenance of a system of nation states would very probably continue to breed the nationalist politics that had been responsible for two world wars in the first half of the twentieth century. However, advocates of constitutional federalism were to see their dreams overtaken by events. Nation states were soon restored to Europe, and advocates of closer integration sought an alternative approach.

This approach was exemplified by the Schuman Plan of 1950 – Robert Schuman was French foreign minister at the time – which led to creation of the ECSC in 1951. This was the forerunner of the EC. The ECSC established a common market in coal and steel, both key areas for industrial economies. However, Schuman planned far more than a mere coal and steel community. He saw the ECSC as a first step on the road to economic and political integration. Schuman hoped that successful integration in one area would create pressure for integration in other areas. For example, a common market for coal and steel would create pressure for broader cooperation in energy policies. This, in turn, would create pressure for cooperation in industrial policies. In this way an initially small step would snow-ball into something much more important.

Students of integration describe this snowballing as a 'spillover effect', with cooperation in one area creating pressure for integration in others. This seemingly inexorable logic is known as *neo-functionalist spillover*.[11] For neo-functionalists, however, spillover means something quite specific. It was expected that spillover effects would be generated at the supranational level with the Commission in the lead. As integration continued, functions that had previously been performed by member states would pass to the supranational level. This 'functional spillover' would also generate a 'political spillover' as there would be a re-focusing of activity, for example by pressure groups, on newly-important supranational institutions. European integration could develop a self-reinforcing dynamic with supranational institutions at the forefront. In time it was also thought that 'geographical spillover' would draw neighbouring states into the developing European Community.

This sounded plausible and appeared to fit EC development in the 1950s and early 1960s. However, the theory no longer seemed applicable in the period from the mid-1960s to the mid-1980s. In 1965 the French President de Gaulle enforced national rights of veto in EC decision-making, thereby reducing the scope of supra-national authority. During the 1970s the EC seemed incapable of acting during severe economic recession. On 20 March 1982 the *Economist*'s front cover showed a tombstone bearing an inscription for the EC. It read:

EEC
Born March 25, 1957
Moribund March 25, 1982
Capax imperii nisi imperasset [it seemed capable of power until it tried to wield it].

At this time the momentum of the integrative process appeared to have dissipated. 'Eurosclerosis' was widely held to have set in. Not surprisingly, neo-functionalist theories fell into obsolescence.

The obsolescence of integration theory?

It has been argued that an erroneous 'end of ideology' assumption underpinned neo-functionalist theory which implied that economic growth would continue unabated, and that the main question facing western societies was how to distribute wealth.[12] Neo-functionalists thought that the best way to do it was by appointing experts – technocrats – at the supranational level who, because of their expertise, would arrive at decisions that were best for everybody. It did not quite work out like that. In the 1970s governments were faced with the problem of coping with both rising unemployment and increasing inflation. Supranational integration was not an option many appeared to consider.

Neo-functionalists were criticised for trying to write nationalism out of the political equation. They thought that nationalist views would be consigned to history, overwhelmed by the logic of integration. Again this was not to be the case. In the 1960s the EC came into conflict with strongly nationalistic Gaullists in France, in the 1980s and 1990s with Thatcherites in Britain. As Wallace writes, 'Politics follows its own logic, not simply those of economics and technology'.[13] Nationalists like Charles de Gaulle and Margaret Thatcher would not be swept along by the 'inexorable logic' of integration.

How then do we explain the resurgence of integration since the mid-1980s? It would seem strange to try to breathe new life into neo-functionalist theory when it appears to have failed to explain events from 1965 until 1984. Analysts have instead pointed to the importance of member states in the process of integration.

'Realist' views

In creating a spillover effect, what matters, 'realists' contend, are the attitudes of member states not the role of supranational institutions. If member states do not want to integrate they will not do so, and there is not much the Commission can do about it. If we take, for example, the resurgence of European integration in the mid-1980s, five factors have been seen as underpinning the resurgence of member states' interest in integration:[14]

- Expanded EC membership, with Greece joining in 1981 and Portugal and Spain in 1986
- Solution of Britain's budget contribution problem in 1984
- Intensification of pressures on member states and business from the international political economy, such as competitive threats from hi-tech industries in the USA and Japan
- Failure of trusted regulatory policies to combat economic recession and the turn to neo-liberal policies of deregulation
- The French Socialist government's abandonment of its reflationary economic policies in 1983 and its move to an austerity programme.

The argument here is that momentum generated at national level through a convergence of preferences favoured European integration. Supranational institutions, such as the Commission under its new president, Jacques Delors, appointed in 1985, may have reacted to this convergence, but they did not create it. In opposition to neo-functionalists who seek creation of an integrative dynamic at supranational level, 'realists' focus on the impetus national governments give to the process. From a realist perspective 'successful spillover requires prior programmatic agreements among governments, expressed in an intergovernmental bargain'.[15]

Postulating an opposition between supranational and intergovernmental approaches to European integration may actually create a false dichotomy. It is clear that member states remain central to the process of European integration and that an understanding of the intergovernmental deals that underpin the landmarks of European integration is essential. At the same time, these deals can create new competences for supranational institutions which allow them a margin of autonomy that weakens member-state control. As Putnam has observed, it may therefore be fruitless to ask whether it is member states or supranational institutions that control the process of European integration because the answer is a rather uninteresting 'both, sometimes'.[16] It is more interesting to explore particular policy issues and the relation between intergovernmentalism and supranationalism underpinning transfers of competence to the EU level. This suggests we should view the transfer of policy competences from national to supranational level as being located along a continuum ranging from intergovernmentalism to supranationalism. Immigration and foreign policy are located at the intergovernmental end of the scale and member states still hold sway. At the supranational end of the scale, where it makes sense to talk of common European policies, are agricultural policy and regional development. In turn, this provides the important insight that it is 'hybridity' – meaning the combination of intergovernmentalism and supranationalism – that is central to an understanding of the development and operation of the EU.

Contrasting perspectives on integration

Britain has traditionally preferred intergovernmental cooperation to integration through supranational arrangements. Whether this preference for intergovernmental cooperation is sustainable in an era when issues such as foreign and security policy and immigration and asylum policy are moving 'closer' to the supranational method remains an open question.

Supranationalism implies a central authority with power over member states, the so-called 'Brussels empire' that alarms Eurosceptics. A federal system would seek to preserve some measure of national and subnational autonomy. The EU already shows signs of federation, albeit a form of 'cooperative federalism' whereby member states and the EU share responsibilities because neither has the authority to tackle the challenges they face on their own.

Explanations of integration are also contrasting. In the 1950s and early 1960s analysts pointed to the dynamic effects of supranational institutions, primarily the Commission, in creating a 'spillover effect' as integration proceeded 'logically' from one sector to another. This view is opposed by those who take a 'realist' view and point to the important role played by member states in determining the speed and direction of integration.

Rather than opposing supranationalism with intergovernmentalism it may be more useful to seek insights from both these approaches. This implies recognition of the importance of member states in determining the scope and pace of European integration; but also acknowledgement that once a decision to integrate has been made then a significant margin of autonomy can be ceded to supranational institutions such as the Commission and Court with the effect that member states no longer control the process.

What is clear is that there has been a remarkable process of political and economic integration in Europe since the Second World War. The chapters that follow look at this process and at Britain's role in it. The next chapter looks at integration in Europe prior to British accession. Britain was distrustful of supranationalism and stayed out of the EEC, thus failing to shape policy priorities that were to prove disadvantageous when it did decide to seek membership.

Notes

1 W Wallace, *The Dynamics of European Integration* (Pinter/Royal Institute of International Affairs, London, 1990), ch 1.

2 E Haas, 'The Study of Regional Integrations: Reflections on the Joy and Anguish of Pretheorizing', in L Lindberg and S Scheingold (eds) *Regional Integration: Theory and Research* (Harvard University Press, Cambridge, Mass, 1971), p6.

3 B Laffan, *Integration and Cooperation in Europe* (Routledge, London, 1992), Introduction.

4 Ibid.

5 F Capotori, 'Supranational Organisations', in R Bernhardt (ed) *Encyclopaedia of Public International Law*, Instalment 5 (Elsevier, Amsterdam, 1983), pp62-8.

6 W Wallace, 'What Price Interdependence? Sovereignty and Interdependence in British Politics', *International Affairs* 62 (1986), p367.

7 M Burgess, *Federalism and Federation in Western Europe* (Croom Helm, London, 1986).

8 K Wheare, *Federal Government* (Oxford University Press, Oxford, 1963).

9 S Bulmer and W Wessels, *The European Council: Decision-Making in European Politics* (Macmillan, London, 1987).

10 J Loughlin, 'Federalism, Regionalism and European Union', *Politics* 13 (1993), pp9-16

11 C Pentland, *International Theory and European Integration* (Faber and Faber, London, 1973).

12 S George, *Politics and Policy in the European Community*, second edition (Oxford University Press, Oxford, 1991), ch 2.

13 Wallace, op cit, p7.

14 R Keohane and S Hoffmann, *The New European Community* (Westview Press, Oxford, 1991), ch 1.

15 R Keohane and S Hoffmann, 'Conclusions: Community Politics and Institutional Change', in Wallace, op cit, p287.

16 R Putnam, 'Diplomacy and Domestic Politics', *International Organization* 42 (1988), pp427-60.

2 Rebuilding Europe

In July 1993 the Tour de France passed the memorial to the thousands killed at Verdun in the First World War. On it flew the flags of France and Germany. Between them fluttered Europe's blue flag with 12 gold stars. This scene symbolised the post-war movement towards integration in Europe as a means of undermining nationalistic enmities. It also illustrated the rapprochement between France and Germany which underpins the European Union. At the end of the Second World War the French sought to incorporate West Germany into a peaceful European order without risking a restoration of German military power which could once again threaten world peace. There was an instrumental motivation for this course of action: subjugation of Germany after the First World War had failed with disastrous consequences. Integration of Germany into the framework of capitalist liberal democracies was seen as a solution to the 'problem' of Germany. This meant supranational structures of government within which members' sovereignty would be 'pooled'. First came the ECSC in 1951. Later, in 1957, came the EEC.

East versus West After the Second World War Europe faced severe economic and political challenges. To the east the Soviet Union consolidated its strength. To the West states looked to their principal ally, the USA, for help. 'Europe had become an object of world politics with the shots being called by the great powers.'[1]

American assistance to Europe came in the form of Marshall Aid, named after Secretary of State George C Marshall who developed the plan to rebuild west European economies. About $13 billion worth of aid was distributed among west European countries between 1948 and 1952. West Germany was the main beneficiary, receiving $4.5 billion. This served to draw it firmly into the Western bloc. By establishing the Organisation for European Economic Cooperation (OEEC) in May 1948, the Americans sought to involve recipient countries in the Marshall Aid distribution process. The British, then the strongest power in Europe, resolutely advocated intergovernmental cooperation in the OEEC rather than institution of supranational structures with powers over member states.

The USA was keen to see the establishment in western Europe of open capitalist economies with liberal-democratic political systems. It made sound commercial sense for the USA to seek to restore the economies of the West because it could then trade with them. It was not only the external threat from the East that perturbed the Americans. There were also strong communist parties in France and Italy. Restoration of economic prosperity within a capitalist order was seen as a defence against communism in these countries.

On Soviet insistence, Marshall Aid was not accepted in eastern Europe. Both Czechoslovakia and Poland rejected it. This, and the Czech communists' seizure of sole power in February 1948, led Britain, the Benelux countries (Belgium, Luxembourg and the Netherlands) and France to form the Brussels Treaty organisation in March 1948 whereby they pledged mutual military aid and economic cooperation. Also in March 1948 the three Western occupying powers in Germany – France, Britain and the USA – unified their occupation zones and convened a constitutional assembly which introduced currency reforms that created the Deutschmark (DM). This caused similar steps to be taken in the east of Germany by the fourth occupying power, the Soviet Union. A Soviet attempt to blockade Berlin in the winter of 1948 was breached by allied airlifts.

In April 1949 NATO was established by the Treaty of Washington. This firmly committed the USA to defence of western Europe. In September 1949 the Federal Republic of Germany (FRG) was created; in October the German Democratic Republic (GDR) was established in the east. The division of Germany provided firm evidence of the iron curtain that had fallen across the continent of Europe.

Inter-governmentalism versus supra-nationalism

The restoration of nation states after the Second World War had dashed the hopes of constitutional federalists who had sought a United States of Europe. In their opinion, only such a dramatic step could transcend the bitterness and divisions that had plagued the continent and generated two world wars in the space of 30 years. Ways forward in a Europe of nation states were unclear.

What was clear was that a basic divide was emerging between Britain on the one hand, and the six countries that were to found the ECSC in 1951 on the other. The British had no intention of participating in a supranational organisation. The Benelux countries had already taken steps towards 'pooling' their sovereignty when, in 1948, they had set up a customs union.

Tensions between supranationalists and intergovernmentalists became apparent at the May 1948 Congress of Europe in The Hague, where more than 700 prominent Europeans met to discuss the future of the continent. The outcome of the meeting was creation of the Council of Europe in May 1949. It was located in Strasbourg, on the Franco-German border, in order to symbolise reconciliation between these two countries. Britain's preference for intergovern-mentalism prevailed in the Council of Europe: decisions in its Council of Ministers are taken on the basis of unanimity. It has come to be identified with the European Convention on Human Rights (ECHR), signed in November 1950. This, after the atrocities of the Second World War, signified a commitment to human rights as binding on sovereign states. By 1998 the Council of Europe had 40 members and was the largest pan-European grouping

Schuman's plan

A core group of west European countries felt frustrated by Britain's suspicion of supranationalism and, as the Benelux countries had already done in their customs union, sought closer structures of eco-nomic integration. It was, and still is, France and (what was then West) Germany that formed the key axis within this supranational integrative project. Plans developed by French foreign minister Robert Schuman were for a common market in coal and steel. The ECSC was an attempt to resolve the question of how to restore German economic prosperity, from which the French would benefit, while binding West Germany to a peaceful west European order.

Schuman's plan, proposed on 9 May 1950, led to creation of the ECSC by the Treaty of Paris in April 1951. It created a common market for coal and steel and supranational structures of government to run the community. Schuman's ambitions were not limited sim-ply to coal and steel. As he put it, 'Europe will not be made all at once or according to a single general plan. It will be built through concrete achievements which first create a de facto solidarity'.[2]

The ECSC broke new ground in two ways:

● It laid the foundations for a common market in the basic raw materials needed by an industrial society
● It was the first European inter-state organisation to show supranational tendencies.

Schuman advocated step-by-step integration. A united Europe was the goal, but it would be achieved through 'spillover' effects (see Chapter 1). A leading ally of Schuman was the Frenchman Jean Monnet who became the first President of the High Authority of the ECSC (the forerunner of the Commission), as well as one of the 'patron saints' of latter-day Euro-enthusiasts.

The ECSC's institutions

Four main institutions were created to operate the ECSC. The institutions of the EU developed on this basis:

● The **High Authority** had two main tasks: to make policy proposals and to ensure that member states complied with their obligations. Member states were not allowed to give subsidies and aids to their national coal and steel industries and restrictive practices were outlawed. The High Authority was more than just a bureaucracy, it also had an important political role. Its nine members were not national representatives, they were intended to advance the purposes of European integration

● The **Council of Ministers** was the legislature of the ECSC. There were six members of the Council, with each member state having one representative. As member states were unwilling to lose complete control over key industries, decisions were often made on the basis of unanimity, which meant that decision-making structures were weak. The Council of Ministers introduced an important element of intergovernmentalism into the ECSC

● The **Common Assembly** was meant to provide a democratic input into the working of the ECSC. However, members of the Assembly were not directly elected, but were chosen from the ranks of national parliamentarians. They had a purely advisory role and possessed no legislative authority

● A **Court of Justice** was established to settle disputes between member states and the ECSC. When members signed the Treaty of Paris they entered into a binding legal commitment. The role of the Court was to interpret ECSC law in the event of disputes, and thus to define the parameters of supranational integration.

Although institution of the ECSC created supranational authority, member states were keen to have the final say in decisions that were taken. They ensured that this happened by making the Council of Ministers the decision-making body of the ECSC. Even today, decision-making power in the EU still resides to a large extent with member states in the Council of Ministers.

Two steps forward, one step back

Hoffmann argues that European integration has tended to falter when it has had to deal with matters of 'high politics', such as foreign affairs and defence, and to prosper when confronted with matters of 'low politics', chiefly trade.[3] In the early 1950s the morale of federalists was raised by the success of the ECSC, and they looked to build on this success by creating a European Defence Community (EDC). This represented a move into the domain of 'high politics'.

In 1950, when leader of the opposition in Britain, Winston Churchill had called for a unified European army acting in cooperation with the United States and Germany. In office, though, Churchill's Conservative government of 1951 to 1955 was as hostile to supranationalism as had been its Labour predecessor. It refused to join the EDC. The French left was also opposed to rearmament of Germany within the EDC. The plan was killed off in August 1954 when it was rejected by the French National Assembly. Instead, in the same month, the West European Union (WEU) was established by the six ECSC members, plus Britain, as the west European, intergovernmental pillar of NATO. The WEU incorporated the vanquished axis powers of Germany and Italy into the collective defence structures of western Europe.

The road to Rome

The WEU was a triumph for intergovernmentalists, but federalists were not deterred and returned their attention to economic integration in an attempt to build on the foundations laid by the 1951 Treaty of Paris. What they sought was a common market, like that set up by the Benelux countries in 1948. In June 1955 a conference of foreign ministers was convened in the Italian coastal town of Messina and a committee led by the Belgian foreign minister, Paul-Henri Spaak, was asked to look at options for further integration.

The British had observer status at the conference but soon made it clear that they were not interested in supranational integration. The Spaak report was considered by a meeting of ECSC foreign ministers in Venice in May 1956. The outcome was two treaties of Rome signed in March 1957: one established the European Economic Community and the other set up the European Atomic Energy Community. Thus, there are three founding treaties of the European Communities – the Treaty of Paris (1951) which set up the ECSC and the two Treaties of Rome (1957) which set up the EEC and Euratom. Subsequent treaties such as the Single European Act (1986), the Maastricht Treaty (1992) and the Amsterdam Treaty (1997) amend the founding Treaties.

The EEC became the predominant organisation. Its founding Treaty was premised on 'an ever closer union of the peoples of Europe'. It abolished trade barriers and customs duties and established a common external tariff, thereby making the EEC a customs union. The EEC was also designed to promote the free movement of workers, goods, services and capital within a common market. The member states transferred to the EEC powers to conclude trading agreements with international organisations on their behalf.

Four main institutions, modelled on those set up to run the ECSC, were created to manage the EC:

● The **Commission** A supranational institution responsible for both policy proposals and implementation
● The **Council of Ministers** The legislative authority
● The **Common Assembly** (now known as the European Parliament). Has a consultative role and no legislative authority
● The **Court of Justice** Umpires matters of dispute relating to EC law. Chapter 4 investigates the operation of these institutions.

The EEC Treaty also made provision for a Common Agricultural Policy. Agriculture was an obvious candidate for a common policy for three main reasons. Firstly, it would have been illogical to leave this important area of economic activity with member states.[4] Second, the EEC and the ECSC addressed a range of industrial issues, such that an agricultural policy was seen as a balance to these concerns. Third, France, with its large agricultural sector, sought protection for its farmers as well as access to markets in other member states. The CAP had three founding principles:

● Common agricultural prices in the EEC
● Common financing (meaning an agricultural budget)
● Community preference over imports.

Much of the Treaty framework was vague and depended on the impetus given by member states. The speed and direction of European integration have depended heavily on collective endeavour.

The British response

Distrustful of supranationalism, the British responded to the EC by instigating EFTA, set up by the Stockholm Convention of July 1959. EFTA was in accord with the British preference for intergovernmentalism. The seven signatories – Denmark, Norway, Sweden, Portugal, Austria, Switzerland and Britain – established a free trade area which brought down barriers to trade between members and sought to keep in touch with EC tariff reductions.

By the early 1960s it had become apparent to the British that EFTA was peripheral to the fast-growing economies of the EC. A powerful trading bloc was emerging on Britain's doorstep from which it was excluded. In the 1960s the EC appeared to be going from success to success as the Common External Tariff was put in place and the CAP established. Britain was forced to re-evaluate its policy, and sought membership of the EC. However, French President de Gaulle was distinctly underwhelmed by the prospect of British membership and, in 1963 and 1967, vetoed British accession bids.

The origins of the European Community

A rapid process of European integration was instigated in the 1950s by institution of the ECSC, the EEC and Euratom. What was distinct about these organisations was their supranational structures. Member states were, though, unwilling to cede complete authority to them. In consequence, the intergovernmental Council of Ministers was made the legislative authority of the Communities.

Supranational integration failed to break into the domain of 'high politics' following rejection of the EDC in 1954. Economic integration has tended to prove easier for the EC to achieve than political integration. Economic interdependence is readily apparent in post-war Europe, and from the ECSC of 1951 to the single market of 1993 structures to manage that interdependence have been created. In the sphere of 'high politics', countries were keen to preserve the right to act in accord with their own national interests. Since the Maastricht Treaty, issues of 'high politics' covering foreign and security policy and interior policies, such as immigration and asylum, have moved closer to European integration.

Britain remained aloof from supranational organisations. However, this was not just the product of its distrust of supranationalism. As the US Secretary of State Dean Acheson put it in 1960, the British had lost an empire and were trying to find a role. By the end of the 1950s a basic divide had emerged in Europe between the 'EC 6' and the 'EFTA 7'. The EU has proved to be the magnet to which EFTA countries have been attracted. By 1998 most of the EFTA member states had joined the EC (Austria, Britain, Denmark, Portugal and Sweden). Norway rejected membership in referendums held in 1972 and 1994, but is associated with the EU through the European Economic Area. Of the original EC and EFTA members only the Swiss have continued to steer clear of supranational integration.

Notes

1 J Story (ed), *The New Europe* (Blackwell, Oxford, 1993), p11.
2 Quoted in N Nugent, *The Government and Politics of the European Community*, second edition (Macmillan, London, 1991), p35.
3 S Hoffmann, 'Obstinate or Obsolete: The Fate of the Nation State and the Case of Western Europe', *Daedalus 95* (1966), pp862-915.
4 In the 1950s and 1960s agriculture was far more central to economic life than it is today. In 1959 24 per cent of the EC's population was employed in the agricultural sector. By 1991 this figure had fallen to 6 per cent, and agriculture accounted for less than 3 per cent of EC GDP.

3 Britain joins the club

British policy towards the EC was re-evaluated in the 1960s. Both Macmillan (between 1961 and 1963) and Wilson (in 1967) pursued membership of the Community, only to be rebuffed by de Gaulle's veto. It was left to Heath to lead Britain into the EC in January 1973. With hindsight it can be argued that Britain stayed out of the Community when it should have joined in the 1950s, and joined when it should have stayed out in the 1970s. Britain spent its first decade of membership arguing about the terms of accession and seeking a budget rebate. After the budget issue had been resolved in June 1984 the British were keen advocates of a single market within which people, goods, services and capital could move freely. Neither Thatcher nor Major was enthusiastic about what other member states saw as the economic and social policy implications of the single market. Tony Blair promised a more constructive engagement with the EU, but beyond the talk of 'modernising' the EU, the central issue of Britain's stance on European Monetary Union (EMU) looms. For this and other reasons, after more than 25 years of EU membership, Britain has acquired the reputation of an 'awkward partner'.[1]

1960s: Britain says Yes, de Gaulle says No

It can be argued that British political élites made three fundamental miscalculations about the EC in the 1950s:[2]

● The British government held the view that supranational integration was foredoomed and that the EC's federalising tendencies would soon founder on the rocks of member states' national concerns. The British refused to join the ECSC and the EDC and only sent a senior civil servant to the Messina negotiations in 1955 which led to the Rome Treaties of 1957. Other countries dispatched eminent politicians
● Britain believed that the problems of the post-war era could be met by establishing a free trade area (EFTA), and that supranational integration was unnecessary
● The British underestimated the obstacles to accession once a distinct course of action had been decided upon.

De Gaulle's vision was of Europe as a third force between the super-powers of East and West, ideally with him as its leader. He thought Britain would seek to dominate the EC and place it firmly in the American bloc. Britain and America shared a 'globalist' perspective, of which central features were commitment to an open world trading order and rejection of protectionism.

Three broad characteristics of British policy towards the EC in the 1950s should be highlighted:

● Aloofness towards Europe based on a perception, as Churchill put it, that Britain was 'with them' against the greater foe of communism, but not 'of them' in participating in integration
● Opposition to the supranational implications of the EC which were seen as eroding national sovereignty. In Britain a sense of national identity had been strengthened by the experience of the Second World War. The sovereignty that had been so keenly defended then was not about to be ceded to supranational institutions in Europe
● Development of an alternative policy focused on the empire and the 'special relationship' with the USA. Europe was seen as one of three interlocking circles, but as third in the order of priorities.

By the early 1960s the British government was questioning its aloofness towards the EC. The 'special relationship' with the USA had been dented by the Suez crisis of 1956, when the USA had declined to support Britain's military intervention in Egypt. It was beginning to seem that the relationship was more special in British eyes than in American, and that post-war hopes of partnership had been replaced by an economic and military dependence by means of which Britain was consigned to a role of 'increasingly impotent avuncularity'.[3]

Britain was also worried that its close ties with America could be supplanted by links between the USA and the EC. The USA feared that de Gaulle's 'third force' aspirations for Europe would weaken the Western alliance, and hoped Britain would steer the EC in the right direction. In July 1962 President Kennedy called for an Atlantic partnership between the USA and the EC, including Britain. He wanted to see an outward-looking and open EC.

In the 1960s the Commonwealth ideal that nations of the former empire could cooperate on an equal footing took several dents. Divisions emerged between the 'black' and 'white' Commonwealth over, for example, Britain's less than wholehearted denunciation of the South African regime after the Sharpeville massacre of 1961. Conflict also arose between India and Pakistan over the disputed territory of Kashmir, and more generally over the unilateral declaration of independence made by Ian Smith's regime in Rhodesia in 1965.

By the time Harold Wilson became prime minister in 1964, economic concerns impelled the membership bid. EFTA was not proving a success when compared to the dynamic economies of the EC, and Commonwealth trading patterns were changing as Australia and

New Zealand looked to markets in the USA and Japan. Wilson had come to office espousing 'the white heat of the scientific revolution' that would modernise the British economy. Larger markets were needed for high technology industries, such as aircraft and computers, but exclusion from the EC meant separation from fast-growing neighbouring economies.

On all usual economic indicators Britain was lagging behind the EC. For example, between 1958 and 1968 real earnings in Britain rose by 38 per cent, compared to 75 per cent in the EC. Fear of isolation is apparent in a memorandum sent by Macmillan to his foreign secretary, Selwyn Lloyd, in 1959:

> For the first time since the Napoleonic era the major continental powers are united in a positive economic grouping, with considerable political aspects, which, although not specifically directed against the United Kingdom, may have the effect of excluding us both from European markets and from consultation in European policy.

1973: membership

In 1969 the political complexion of the two countries at the heart of European integration – France and West Germany – changed in a way advantageous to Britain's membership hopes. In France President de Gaulle resigned and was replaced by Georges Pompidou, who favoured British accession. In West Germany the new Social Democratic government, led by Willy Brandt, was also keen to see enlargement of the EC.

Prior to the accession of new member states the founder members laid down a budgetary framework for the Community at a heads of government meeting in The Hague in 1969. This was formalised by Treaty in 1970. This provided a classic example of rules that were not to Britain's advantage being determined in the absence of any input from the British government. When Britain did join it was obliged to accept what is known as the *acquis communautaire*, including the budgetary arrangements. Construction of the EC's 'own resources' was not to Britain's advantage as it effectively penalised countries with extensive trading links outside the EC. When goods from outside the EC enter a member state they face the EC's common external tariff which, after collection, becomes part of the Community's 'own resources'. Having substantial trading links with non-EC countries, notably those in the Commonwealth, Britain was disadvantaged from the start by this measure. In addition, Britain, with a relatively efficient agricultural sector, has never gained much profit from the main financial activity of the EC, farm price support.

Negotiations on British accession began in June 1970 under Conservative prime minister Edward Heath. In July 1971 a White Paper was published. It noted some of the disadvantages of membership:

● It was estimated that food prices would go up by 15 per cent over a six-year period because the CAP contained a system of Community preference which would mean that Britain could no longer shop around on cheaper world food markets

● Increased food prices would contribute to a 3 per cent increase in the cost of living over a six-year period

● British contributions to the EC budget would amount to £300 million a year, making Britain the second largest contributor behind West Germany. British contributions would be high because it had extensive external trading links.

Britain joined the EC on 1 January 1973, along with Denmark and Ireland. (Norway also negotiated accession terms but the Norwegian people rejected membership in a referendum.) Although Heath was pursuing a policy developed by his predecessors, who had come to the conclusion that EC membership was necessary if Britain was not to risk economic and political isolation, he was more than merely a pragmatic European. Indeed, Heath was in the 1970s a keen advocate of membership and is still a convinced euro enthusiast. He also of course realised that on pragmatic grounds Britain had little option but to enter the EC and try to shape it from within. On 28 October 1971 MPs voted by 356 to 244 in favour of accession to the Community. The Conservatives were allowed a free vote while Labour imposed a three-line whip against accession. In the event 69 Labour MPs voted in favour of joining the Community.

British accession occurred just as the economies of western Europe were ending their long post-war period of economic growth. Britain could hardly have chosen a less propitious moment to dip a tentative toe into the waters of supranational economic and political integration. Oil price increases soon helped to plunge the British and European economies into recession.

1974-75: renegotation and referendum

For Harold Wilson Britain's membership of the EC posed something of a dilemma. He had sought accession as prime minister in the 1960s, but in Britain's adversarial political system he could not pass up the chance of picking up a stick with which to beat the Conservative government. What Wilson did was oppose the terms of accession – as negotiated by Heath – and pledge a future Labour government to renegotiation and a referendum.

After Labour returned to power in February 1974 renegotiation talks were led by Foreign Secretary James Callaghan. Britain gained little through renegotiation that it could not have gained through normal Community channels. Furthermore, the degree of acrimony engendered by the bargaining soured Britain's relations with other members for many years. The House of Commons endorsed the renegotiated terms by 396 votes to 170 in April 1975. Ominously for the Labour government, and despite pro-Community speeches from both Wilson and Callaghan, a special Labour conference on 26 April 1975 voted by 3.7 million to 1.9 million to leave the EC.

The pledge to hold a referendum helped Wilson overcome divisions within the Labour Party. Indeed, it seems likely that this was its major purpose. During the referendum campaign of 1975 Wilson suspended the convention of collective cabinet responsibility so that cabinet ministers could speak according to their consciences. The 'Yes' campaign commanded powerful political assets despite opinion polls at the outset pointing to a 'No' vote. It had strong support from Fleet Street and from powerful business interests which provided a large part of the £1.5 million spent in the quest for an affirmative vote. It also gathered a powerful coalition of centrist politicians, including Heath, Labour's Roy Jenkins and Liberal leader Jeremy Thorpe. By comparison, the 'No' campaign raised just £133,000. It found itself outgunned and was weakened by its disparate character: Tony Benn from the left of the Labour Party formed a decidedly uneasy temporary alliance with right-wingers such as Enoch Powell. The outcome, on 5 June 1975, was a two to one vote in favour of continued membership on a 64 per cent turnout.[4]

1976-79: Callaghan's difficulties

In April 1976 James Callaghan succeeded Harold Wilson as prime minister and inherited a Labour Party divided over EC membership. Labour's rank and file distrusted the EC even though some prominent Labour politicians, such as Roy Jenkins and Shirley Williams, were keen advocates of membership. There were two main areas of concern. Firstly, it was felt that integration into a supranational community would restrict national sovereignty and the freedom of action of a Labour government. Second, the EC was seen as a 'capitalist club' with market-based purposes that offered little to working people. Arguments over EC membership were symptomatic of a deeper malaise within the Labour Party which saw the leadership frequently at odds with the membership and culminated in right-wingers splitting to form the Social Democratic Party (SDP) in January 1981.

In February 1975 the Conservatives replaced Edward Heath as leader with Margaret Thatcher. Thatcher had opposed the 1975 referendum describing it, in a phrase that would haunt her in her Eurosceptical dotage when she called for a referendum on Maastricht, as a device for demagogues. She argued for a 'Yes' vote on the grounds that Britain needed to foster economic links with Europe.

Prime Minister Callaghan was also a pragmatist and an Atlanticist who held no truck with the lofty rhetoric of European union. He had a poor reputation in EC circles as a result of his dogged pursuit of national interests during the British renegotiation, and failed as premier to ease tensions caused by Britain's entry to the Community.

From March 1977 Callaghan relied on support from the Liberals to sustain his administration. This support was conditional on insertion of a clause introducing proportional representation (PR) as the method of voting in direct elections to the European Parliament. Such a clause was duly inserted into the European Assembly Elections Bill of 1977. However, it provoked a cabinet revolt and, on a free vote in the House of Commons, was defeated. It also delayed direct elections which, to the irritation of other member states, were put back from 1978 to 1979.

The British presidency of the EC in the first six months of 1977 did little to enhance Britain's reputation. Callaghan was hamstrung by a Eurosceptical party and by domestic economic problems. In a letter to the General Secretary of the Labour Party at the start of the British presidency he outlined three basic principles that informed the Labour government's stance on the EC:

● Maintenance of the authority of EC nation states and national parliaments, with no increase in the powers of the European Parliament
● Emphasis on the necessity for national governments to achieve their own economic, regional and industrial objectives
● Reform of the budget procedure.

Contained within these policy principles is a clear restatement of Britain's suspicion of supranationalism and continued concern over the high level of budget contributions. These concerns were shared by Margaret Thatcher when she became prime minister in May 1979. She battled for a budget rebate and opposed extensions of supranational authority, but Britain's reputation as an 'awkward partner' both preceded and has survived her.

British membership was advocated on pragmatic economic grounds. Britain thought it was joining a common market – an economic organisation – and played down the political consequences. Prime Minister Heath rejected the idea that Britain was joining a putative federation. Pragmatic acceptance of membership means that Britain has tended to judge the EC by utilitarian standards: what does it have to pay and what does it get out of it? Britain was paying a lot in the late 1970s and early 1980s and seemed to be getting little in return. Not surprisingly, enthusiasm for the EC did not run deep.

1979-84: the budget rebate

Margaret Thatcher inherited the policy concerns of preceding Labour governments, particularly over the high level of contributions to the EC budget. By the end of the 1970s Britain was the second largest contributor to the budget and was in danger of becoming the largest, paying more than £1 billion a year, even though it had the third-lowest GDP per capita of the nine member states.

A series of often acrimonious negotiations was held between 1979 and 1984. Then Commission President, Roy Jenkins, writes in his memoirs of long hours spent discussing the BBQ: the British Budget Question, or as he preferred, the Bloody British Question. He notes how Thatcher made a bad start at the Strasbourg summit in 1979 when she had a strong case but succeeded in alienating other leaders upon whose support she depended for a deal to be struck. Britain's partners were unwilling to receive lectures on the issue from Thatcher and were alienated by suggestions that the budget mechanisms were tantamount to theft of British money, particularly as Britain had known the budgetary implications when it had joined.[5]

The issue was finally resolved at the Fontainebleau summit in June 1984 when a rebate was agreed amounting to 66 per cent of the difference between Britain's VAT contributions to the budget and its receipts. The scheme has been in operation since 1985 and generated a British rebate of about Ecu one billion a year.

This agreement was important as it meant the leaders of the Community could lift their sights from interminable squabbles over the budget and begin to think strategically about the future of the Community. The British government's preferences had been clearly stated in a paper entitled 'Europe: The Future', circulated at the Fontainebleau summit.[6] The paper called for the attainment by 1990 of a single market within which goods, services, people and capital could move freely. It very clearly reflected the deregulatory zeal which Thatcher brought to domestic politics.

In Britain Thatcher had sought to 'roll back the frontiers of the state' and allow free enterprise and market forces to flourish. Thatcherism embodied what has been characterised as the amalgam of the free economy and the strong state.[7] For Thatcherites the EC was a stultifying bureaucracy that could do with a dose of Thatcherite free market vigour, whether it liked it or not.

To secure the single market promoted in the Fontainebleau paper Britain needed allies among its EC partners, and there were potential ones at both the national and supranational level:

● The two key member states, France and West Germany, were amenable to single market reforms. The French Socialist government elected in 1981 had been forced to abandon its reflationary economic policies in 1983, and the Christian Democrat-led coalition of Chancellor Kohl in West Germany supported creation of a single market
● New Commission President, Jacques Delors, took office in 1985 and seized upon the single market as his 'big idea' to restart integration and shake off the 'Eurosclerosis' of the 1970s and early 1980s. Delors was assisted in his ambitions by the Commissioner responsible for the internal market, former Conservative Cabinet Minister Lord Cockfield.

A White Paper prepared by the Commission put forward 300 legislative proposals for the single market. These were later whittled down to a mere 282. The proposals were accepted by heads of government at the Milan summit in June 1985. In the face of objections from the Danes, Greeks and British, an intergovernmental conference was convened to consider reform of the EC's decision-making process to accompany the single market plan.

While Britain was hostile to strengthening Community institutions, France and West Germany asserted that attainment of the single market in fact necessitated increased powers for supranational institutions such as the European Parliament to ensure that decision-making efficiency and a measure of democratic accountability followed the transfer of authority to the supranational level. The British did not see it that way and thought the single market could be achieved without reform of the EC's institutional structure. The result was a compromise package: the 1986 Single European Act (SEA). This had two main features:

● Establishment of a target date, the end of 1992, for completion of the internal market and attainment of the 'four freedoms': freedom of movement of people, goods, services and capital
● Strengthening of EC institutional structures, with qualified majority

voting (QMV) introduced in the Council of Ministers covering new policy areas relating to harmonisation measures necessary to achieve the single market. Increased use of QMV ensured swifter decision-making. Unanimity was still required for fiscal policy, the free movement of persons and employees' rights legislation. The European Parliament's role was strengthened by introduction of the 'cooperation procedure' which gave power to suggest amendments to Community legislation. The Council retained the right to reject Parliament's amendments (see Chapter 4).

The White Paper put forward by the Commission identified three kinds of barriers to trade that needed to come down if the single market was to be attained:

● **Physical barriers** Mainly customs and immigration controls
● **Fiscal barriers** Indirect taxes vary in the Community and constitute a barrier to trade
● **Technical barriers** These were very significant because member states had developed their own product standards which differed widely and formed a substantial barrier to free trade.

The British government objected to large parts of the White Paper. With regard to removal of physical barriers, it had long been concerned to prevent free movement of people, fearing the implications of the relaxation of external frontier controls and passport checks for terrorism, drugs trafficking and illegal immigration. However, in June 1989 a meeting of EC interior ministers in Palma advocated intergovernmental cooperation on these issues. Indeed, a core group of member states had already made significant steps in the direction of free movement of people. On 14 June 1985 at Schengen in Luxembourg, West Germany, France and the Benelux countries signed an agreement gradually to abolish all frontier controls between them. By 1998 only the UK and Ireland remained outside of Schengen.

Significant problems were faced in the sphere of technical barriers. Required to eliminate barriers to free trade, the Commission found itself teetering on the edge of the regulatory nightmare of having to define what constituted particular products so that common standards could exist across the Community. In the event, it got round the problem by using a 1979 ECJ decision over the French liqueur Cassis de Dijon to establish the important principle of mutual recognition. The original dispute had been between France and West Germany over the level of alcoholic content necessary to a liqueur: by German standards, Cassis did not qualify. The ECJ ruled that if a product is legally produced in one member state then it can be legally sold in another, provided that matters like public safety in the importing country are satisfied.

The benefits of a single European market were claimed to be substantial. A 1988 study, *The Costs of Non-Europe*, found that savings to business and commerce through removal of barriers could be in the region of Ecu 200 billion, corresponding to a potential annual growth rate of about 5 per cent. The report claimed that within five years of completion the internal market could generate five million new jobs.[8] In fact, the 1992 target date coincided with economic recession and increased levels of unemployment across the EU.

A particular problem has been realisation of free movement for people because of the sensitivities of some member states about the relaxation of frontier controls. From 1 January 1993 people, goods, services and capital were supposed to be able to move freely within the EC. The divisions over the relaxation of controls on the free movement of people prompted the Schengen agreement. Britain refused to participate in Schengen because it wished to maintain its external frontier controls. Ireland was unable to participate because of the Common Travel Area it shares with the UK which would be jeopardised by Schengen accession. Denmark, too, although a Schengen member opted-out of moves towards supranationalisation of free movement, immigration and asylum.

In 1998 the second edition of the Commission's single market scoreboard showed that member states had implemented all but 249 (18.2 per cent) of the 1368 Single Market Directives. Some member states (Austria, Sweden, Finland, Germany and Greece) had made better progress than others (Belgium, Italy, Portugal, Luxembourg and France). Finland came top with 98.8 per cent implementation, the UK had implemented 96.2 per cent of directives to rank sixth, while Belgium lay in fifteenth and last place with 92.9 per cent of directives implemented.

1987-90: Thatcher's last hurrah

The final years of Margaret Thatcher's premiership were characterised by an almost incessant battle against spillover effects generated by the SEA. For the French and Germans, who had been key single market allies, adoption of a plan to complete the single market was a new beginning for integration. They sought to consolidate the success of the SEA by promoting integration in other areas. Plans were hatched for economic and monetary union (EMU) and for Community social policies to ensure minimum rights for workers in the wake of the freedoms given to capital by the SEA (for further details on both policy areas see Chapter 5).

Thatcher firmly set herself against the integrative consequences of the SEA. As she languished in the opinion polls in 1990 her perceived anti-Europeanism was seen as an electoral liability and was one of the factors which precipitated the challenge to her leadership. The final straw for her opponents came in November 1990 when her former chancellor and foreign secretary, Sir Geoffrey Howe, bitterly criticised her leadership style. Howe's speech was the beginning of the end for Thatcher's premiership, although her successor, John Major, was perceived as the inheritor of the Thatcherite mantle, not least by Thatcher herself.

1990-97: Major, Maastricht and Conservative rebels

Within the EC John Major adopted a more emollient tone than his predecessor and expressed the intention of placing Britain 'at the heart of Europe'. But within Major's vision of the Community, made manifest by his negotiation of the Maastricht Treaty in December 1991, were distinct policy continuities with his predecessor:

● An opt-out from the Social Chapter
● The right for the British Parliament to decide whether Britain would enter the third stage of the plan for EMU when a single currency would be introduced
● Promotion of the notion of subsidiarity, which, in the eyes of the Conservative government, was a way of reinforcing national perspectives on Community decision-making
● Advocacy of intergovernmental cooperation rather than supranational integration in foreign, defence and interior policy. Intergovernmental 'pillars' were built into the Maastricht Treaty.

Unconstrained by high office, Thatcher remarked that she would never have signed the Maastricht Treaty. However, the Treaty Major negotiated and signed could be seen to reflect inherited policy preferences. In addition, Major also reaped the integrative whirlwind Prime Minister Thatcher had helped initiate when she signed the SEA in 1986.

Major's deal at Maastricht temporarily assuaged Tory divisions over Europe and helped lay the foundations for his April 1992 general election victory. A conspicuous feature of the election campaign was lack of debate about Britain's place in the EC. Both Conservative and Labour party managers knew their parties to be divided on the issue, and tacitly conspired to keep silent about it. Eurosceptics were thus not entirely unjustified in later complaining that the British people had not in fact endorsed Maastricht at the 1992 general election, and that they should therefore be allowed a referendum on the issue.

Safely returned to government, Conservative divisions over Europe could not be hidden. A small and determined band of Eurosceptics frequently defied the government by calling for a referendum on Maastricht and trying to block passage of the Maastricht Bill through the House of Commons. The Eurosceptics' rebellion culminated in July 1993 when they contributed to a government defeat on a Labour amendment incorporating the Social Chapter into the Maastricht Treaty. This was a mischievous move by Tory Euro-rebels who hated the Social Chapter, but loathed the Maastricht Treaty even more. Major's response was to 'go nuclear' and turn the issue of Maastricht into one of confidence in the government. In the face of near-certain defeat in a general election and the return of a pro-European Labour government, most of the Tory rebels returned to the party fold.

This did little to ease divisions within the Conservative Party, which reached into the Cabinet. In an unguarded moment during preparation for a television interview, Major referred to three of his Cabinet colleagues as 'bastards' because of their opposition to his EU policies. In June 1995 Major attempted to 'lance the boil', as he put it, by resigning the party leadership and inviting challengers to step forward. Secretary of State for Wales John Redwood stood against Major and although defeated secured 89 votes with a further 22 Conservative MPs abstaining.

During the 1997 general election campaign, the deep divisions within the Conservative Party became all too evident. Even ministers distanced themselves from the party's policy to 'negotiate and decide' (more commonly known as 'wait and see') on EMU. Major felt powerless to dismiss the dissenting ministers because of the effects he feared such action would have on an already damaged party.[9]

In 1992, Major had left the Maastricht negotiating chamber claiming 'game, set and match' for Britain. With hindsight, this appears a rather rash judgement. Instead, the Maastricht deal lit the blue touch paper beneath the Conservative Party which ignited to cause civil war within the party. It played an important part in Labour's landslide victory of May 1997.

'Modernisation' under Labour

One of the main reasons Labour won such a convincing victory in the 1997 general election was the catastrophic division within the Conservative Party caused by the European issue. In office, Labour has shown a determination to avoid such turmoil by maintaining very tight party discipline.

Throughout the election campaign, Labour pledged to establish a more constructive relationship with other EU member states. There was very little substantive difference between the two main parties on the EU. The election manifestos were strikingly similar. Labour was eager to neutralise EU issues that arose during the campaign. For instance, when fish quotas became a salient concern the Conservatives threatened to block Union business if British interests were neglected, Labour immediately said it would do the same.

Labour's victory and the vigour of the new administration attracted interest from across Europe. Almost immediately after the election, Labour signed up to the Social Chapter, as it had pledged to do in its manifesto. The commitment to EU social policy is more ambivalent than it may at first appear because Labour is also committed to forms of labour market flexibility that may call into question aspects of the social model evident in other member states. On the most substantive issue facing the EU – economic and monetary union and the introduction of a single currency – Labour has ruled out participation during the lifetime of the Parliament elected in 1997, although Chancellor Gordon Brown announced in November 1997 that there were no constitutional obstacles to accession. He outlined five economic criteria to be satisfied before entry could occur. These are assessed in more detail in Chapter 5.

British pragmatism in Europe

Pragmatism rather than idealism has shaped Britain's relations with the EU. Britain was distrustful, and to some extent still is, of supranationalism. Policy has tended to be continuous between Labour and Conservative governments. For all the distinctiveness of her style, Margaret Thatcher in fact pursued similar European polices to her Labour predecessor James Callaghan, her Conservative successor John Major continued to follow them. Whether Tony Blair can alter these relationships depends on the difficult balancing act of affecting attitudinal change towards European integration in the UK while convincing other EU member states of Britain's seriousness of purpose as a constructive EU member state rather than a hesitant, and sometimes awkward, observer from the sidelines.

British membership was advocated to avoid political and economic isolation. It was, in effect, a recognition of Britain's reduced status in world affairs as it declined from superpower status to that of a middle-ranking regional power. By not joining in the 1950s or 1960s Britain missed the opportunity to shape key institutions and policies. Policies established in important areas, such as agriculture and the budget, were not to Britain's advantage. When it did join it was soon involved in acrimonious arguments over matters like the budget contribution. Are the same mistakes being made in relation to EMU? Britain has decided to observe from the wings while the other member states establish a single currency. British reluctance meant, for instance, that it was out of the running as the location for the European Central Bank, which will be based in Frankfurt.

The result of British pragmatism has often been isolation in Union circles and apparent cultivation of a reputation for awkwardness. In the 1980s Britain embraced the notion of a single European market with gusto as it mirrored domestic policy preferences. The British Conservative government, though, was soon to find itself at odds with other Community members over the 'spillover' consequences of the SEA. The issue of sovereignty became central to British debate. The next chapter investigates Community institutions and assesses how power actually is distributed within the EU.

Notes

1 S George, *An Awkward Partner: Britain in the European Community* (Oxford University Press, Oxford, 1989).

2 M Beloff, *The Intellectual in Politics, and Other Essays* (Weidenfeld and Nicolson, London, 1970).

3 G Edwards, 'Britain and Europe', in *Story*, op cit, ch 8.

4 On the referendum see A King, *Britain Says Yes: The 1975 Referendum on the Common Market* (American Enterprise Institute, Washington, DC, 1977), and D Butler and U Kitzinger, *The 1975 Referendum* (Macmillan, London, 1976).

5 R Jenkins, *A Life at the Centre* (Macmillan, London, 1991), p495.

6 HM Government, 'Europe: The Future', *Journal of Common Market Studies* 23 (1984), pp74-81.

7 A Gamble, *The Free Economy and the Strong State: The Politics of Thatcherism* (Macmillan, London, 1988).

8 P Cecchini, *1992: The Benefits of a Single Market* (Gower, Aldershot, 1988).

9 A Geddes, 'Europe: Major's Nemesis?', in A Geddes and J Tonge (eds) *Labour's Landslide: The British General Election 1997* (Manchester University Press, Manchester, 1997), pp85-97.

4 Institutions of the European Union

EU institutions hold powers that have increasing impact on the lives of citizens in a number of policy areas. Before moving to look at these policy areas in detail, this chapter investigates EU decision-making processes. Community institutions can appear rather dull and their procedures arcane, but this should not disguise the intensely political and, at times, controversial nature of their roles and responsibilities.

The Brussels empire

There are five main EU institutions:

● **The Commission** Neo-functionalist theorists saw this as a potential driving force of integration and it has, particularly from the outset of the presidency of Jacques Delors in 1985, entered the political demonology of Eurosceptics
● **The Council of Ministers** The legislative authority of the Community in which national governments are represented
● **The European Parliament** The only Community institution which is directly elected
● **The European Court of Justice** Interprets the growing body of Community law and rules on the acts of institutions
● **The European Council** Convened at summit meetings of heads of government.

A characteristic of the EU is its hybridity, that is, the amalgam of intergovernmentalism and supranationalism. Because member states have sometimes been unwilling to cede too much authority to supra-national institutions, such as the European Parliament and the Commission, member states have preserved an important input into EU decision-making structures through intergovernmental forums, such as the Council of Ministers and the European Council.

In the 1980s and 1990s the resurgence of integration has strength-ened supranationalism. Many argue that this creates a 'democratic deficit': EU institutions seem distant from ordinary people and are rarely understood by them. By this reckoning democracy and accountability have been casualties as powers ceded to the Union have tended to fall in a grey area between the control of democratic institutions at either national or supranational level.

The Commission

Following ratification of the Maastricht Treaty in November 1993 the Commission held office for two years until 1995. Thereafter it was decided that the appointment of a new Commission would coincide with elections to the European Parliament (held every five years). The Maastricht Treaty stated that each new Commission must receive the assent of the European Parliament before it can take office. Approval is sought for the Commission en bloc, not for individual commissioners. A new Commission took office in 1995, following the 1994 elections to the European Parliament. It was led by a new President, Jacques Santer, former prime minister of Luxembourg, who replaced Jacques Delors.

The Commission's two main roles are to make policy proposals to the Council of Ministers and to manage implementation of policies once they have been agreed by the Council. Since the 1996 intergovernmental conference (IGC), which developed the main themes of the Amsterdam Treaty, the Commission's work programme has been centred around 'Agenda 2000' which concentrates on preparations for an enlarged Community and sketches the way forward until the end of 2006. Agenda 2000 identifies six key themes: employment, completion of preparations for the euro, enlargement of the Union into central, eastern and southern Europe, the future of the budget framework, the encouragement of coherent Union action at a global level, and building a Europe closer to its citizens with emphasis on public health and quality of life.

The Commission also has rule-making powers for aspects of technical and administrative law not covered by the Treaties. It makes about 4000 to 5000 of these rules every year. In addition, it is responsible for management of Union finances (Ecu 94.4 billion/£63.5 billion in 1998).

Front-line policy implementation is a further key Commission role. An important constraint is the relatively small size of the Commission compared to national bureaucracies, which means that it cannot act alone to ensure compliance with EU policies and relies heavily on cooperation with national bureaucracies. Whether EU law is properly implemented depends to a large extent on how efficient national bureaucracies are in taking account of the various directives and regulations that emanate from Brussels. Regulations are binding in their entirety and directly applicable to all member states. A directive can also be issued which is binding as to the results to be achieved, but the form and method of implementation are left up to the member states. Recommendations, decisions and opinions are also issued but they are not binding on member states.

In addition to making proposals and attempting to implement policy, the Commission must guard the legal framework and ensure that the Treaties and Community law are respected. If it spots infringement the first thing it does is issue a letter of formal notice. This usually suffices, but if compliance does still not occur the Commission can deliver a reasoned opinion. The final recourse is to refer the case to the ECJ. In 1997 the Commission instigated infringement proceedings in 1422 cases (1142 in 1996). In 1997 331 reasoned opinions were issued (435 in 1996). In the same year 121 cases were referred to the Court of Justice (92 in 1996). Italy topped the league table of sinners with 20 references, closely followed by Germany with 19 and Belgium with 18. The UK was referred to the Court on one occasion.

The European Court of Justice has powers to fine offending parties. In April 1986 a price-fixing cartel led by Montedison, ICI, Shell and Hoechst was fined Ecu 55 million (£35 million) by the ECJ. Article 143 of the Maastricht Treaty gave the Court power to impose fines on member states which do not comply with their Treaty obligations. In 1998 Belgium faced fines of £121,000 a day if it did not implement the EU directive on allowing EU citizens from other member states to vote in local elections.

The Commission also has external responsibilities in some policy areas, such as the world trade talks. Here member states have ceded authority to the Union. The external trade profile of the EU is much more highly developed than its external political profile. Trade relations are highly supranationalised while the EU's foreign and security policy arrangements remain largely intergovernmental.

The Commission met 48 times in 1997. It issued 555 proposals, recommendations or draft instruments. The Council adopted 52 directives, 238 regulations, 245 decisions and 14 recommendations. The Commission also issued 238 communications, memorandums and reports covering various policy issues.

Who's who

There are 20 Commissioners: two each from the five largest countries (Britain, France, Germany, Italy and Spain) and one from each of the rest (Table 4.1). Article 158 of the Treaty of Rome stated that: 'The members of the Commission shall be appointed by common accord of the Governments of the member states'. Their appointment is actually determined by heads of government of the member states. Countries which can appoint two Commissioners tend to appoint one from each of the two leading political parties.

The current British Commissioners are former Conservative Cabinet Minister Sir Leon Brittan and the former leader of the Labour Party, Neil Kinnock. The President of the Commission is responsible for allocation of portfolios, although larger and more powerful member states expect to see their Commissioners in prestigious posts.

Table 4.1 | **Commission of the European Communities, 1995–March 1999**

Jacques Santer	President
Sir Leon Brittan	External economic relations with North America, Australia, New-Zealand, Japan, China, Korea, Hong Kong, Macao and Taiwan
	Common commercial policy
	Relations with OECD and WTO
Manuel Marin	External economic relations with Southern Mediterranean countries, the Middle East, Latin America and Asia, including development aid
Martin Bangemann	Industrial affairs
	Information and telecommunications technologies
Karel Van Miert	Competition
Hans van den Broek	External relations with the countries of central and eastern Europe, the former Soviet Union, Mongolia, Turkey, Cyprus, Malta and other European Countries
	Common foreign and security policy and human rights
Jaïo de Deus Pinheiro	External relations with African, Caribbean and Pacific countries and South Africa, Lomé Convention
Padraig Flynn	Employment and social affairs
Marcelino Oreja	Relations with the European Parliament
	Relations with the Members States
Anita Gradin	Immigration, home affairs and justice
	Financial control and fraud prevention
Edith Cresson	Science, research and development
	Human resources, education, training and youth
Ritt Bjerregaard	Environment
Monika Wulf-Mathies	Regional policies
	Cohesion Fund
Neil Kinnock	Transport (including trans-European networks)
Mario Monti	Internal Market, financial services and financial integration
	Customs
	Taxation
Franz Fischler	Agriculture and rural development
Emma Bonino	Fisheries
	Consumer policy
	European Community Humanitarian Office (ECHO)
Yves-Thibault de Silguy	Economic and financial affairs
	Monetary matters
Erkki Liikanen	Budget
Christos Papoutsis	Energy and Euratom Supply Agency

Article 153 of the Treaty of Rome stated that Commissioners should be independent of their national governments in the conduct of their duties, although it is seen as no bad thing if they do keep in touch with domestic political developments as a means of assessing their potential impact on Union decision-making.

Table 4.2 | **Principal administrative units in the Commission, 1998**

Secretariat-General of the Commission
Inspectorate-General
Legal Service
Spokesman's Service
Joint Interpreting and Conference Service
Statistical Office
Translation Service
Informatics Directorate

DG I	External relations: commercial policy and relations with North America, the Far East, Australia and New Zealand
DG IA	External relations: Europe and the New Independent States, Common Foreign and Security Policy and external missions
DG IB	External relations: Southern Mediterranean, TOP and Near East, Latin America, South and South-East Asia and North-South Cooperation
DG II	Economic and financial affairs
DG III	Industry
DG IV	Competition
DG V	Employment, industrial relations and social affairs
DG VI	Agriculture
DG VII	Transport
DG VIII	Development
DG IX	Personnel and administration
DG X	Information, communication, culture, audiovisual
DG XI	Environment, nuclear safety and civil protection
DG XII	Science, research and development, joint research centre
DG XIII	Telecommunications, information market and exploitation of research
DG XIV	Fisheries
DG XV	Internal market and financial services
DG XVI	Regional policies and cohesion
DG XVII	Energy
DG XIX	Budgets
DG XXI	Customs and indirect taxation
DG XXII	Education, training and youth
DG XXIII	Enterprise policy, distributive trades, tourism and co-operatives
DG XXIV	Consumer policy and consumer health protection

European Community Humanitarian Office
Euratom Supply Agency
Office for Official Publications of the European Communities

In 1997 the Commission had an established permanent staff of 16,014, plus 3558 in permanent research posts, with others used on a freelance or expert basis. The notion of a 'Brussels empire' administered by a vast, faceless Commission is rendered rather absurd when the Commission is compared with national bureaucracies. It employs fewer people than the French Ministry of Culture and the British Lord Chancellor's Department, neither of which is a major department of state. It is smaller than the governments of cities like Amsterdam and Madrid.

The Commission is divided into 24 Directorates General, each covering a specific policy area (Table 4.2). DG IX (Personnel and Administration) is the largest, employing about 2500 people. Then DG XII (Science, Research and Development), with 1900 people. DG VI (Agriculture) is the third largest with more than 800 officials.

It is important to note that the Commission is more than simply the EU's bureaucracy. It also plays an important political role. It may not have fulfilled the aspirations of neo-functionalists who, in the 1950s, saw it as leading the way towards a United States of Europe. Nevertheless, in the 1980s, it was instrumental in the resurgence of integration. It was a Commission White Paper which contained the plans for the single market, and the Commission has also pushed hard for EMU and the social dimension.[1]

The Council of Ministers

The Council of Ministers is the EU's legislative authority. It has 15 members, one from each member state. In reality there is not a Council of Ministers but a series of Councils depending on which policy area is being discussed. The three areas covered most frequently by Council meetings are foreign affairs (known as the General Council), economics and finance (ECOFIN) and agriculture, which meet once a month. By contrast, the transport, environment and industry Councils meet between two and four times a year.

As the Council of Ministers is the legislative authority of the Union its decision-making procedures are very important. A reliance upon unanimity was seen as a block on decision-making, while the shift towards majority voting was viewed as essential to the resurgence of integration. Since the Single European Act there has been a shift towards qualified majority voting, which has been reinforced by the Maastricht and Amsterdam Treaties. Key areas of 'high politics', such as foreign and security policy and immigration and asylum, remain subject to unanimity for the time being.

A move towards QMV accompanied the resurgence of integration in the 1980s. Article 100A of the SEA introduced a new legislative procedure – the cooperation procedure – for 10 policy areas, largely related to completion of the single market. Qualified majorities are based on a system of weighted votes (Table 4.3). Qualified majority voting means that one country alone cannot block a piece of legislation covered by majority voting procedures. A blocking minority would usually require a coalition of two big states and two smaller ones. In the 1980s and 1990s increased use of QMV has been seen as a way of unblocking decision-making procedures and ensuring attainment of the single market and other Union goals. In 1997 the Council adopted 48 legislative acts by QMV.

Amsterdam did not greatly extend the range of issues covered by QMV. Prior to negotiation of the Treaty there were more than 60 policy areas where unanimity applied. The proposed number of switches from unanimity to QMV was reduced from 19 in the proposals for Treaty reform prepared by the Irish Presidency, to 11 in the first Dutch text, to five in the final version.

Table 4.3 | **Distribution of weighted votes in the Council of Ministers, 1998**

Germany, France, Italy, United Kingdom	10 votes
Spain	8 votes
Belgium, Greece, Netherlands, Portugal	5 votes
Austria, Sweden	4 votes
Denmark, Finland, Ireland	3 votes
Luxembourg	2 votes

A qualified majority for a Commission proposal requires 62 votes out of a total 87

Before Commission proposals go to the Council of Ministers they are considered by the Committee of Permanent Representatives (COREPER), comprised of member states' diplomatic representatives who seek to oil the wheels of decision making. In many cases preliminary agreements are reached in COREPER and the Council of Ministers acts as a rubber stamp. The Council of Ministers is also serviced by a General Secretariat employing more than 2000 people.

The country holding the Presidency of the Union, which changes every six months, chairs the Council of Ministers. The office of president is held in turn by each member state for a period of six months, in the order shown in Table 4.4:

Table 4.4 | **Presidencies of the European Union, 1998-2003**

	January-June	July-December
1998	United Kingdom	Austria
1999	Germany	Finland
2000	Portugal	France
2001	Sweden	Belgium
2002	Spain	Denmark
2003	Greece	

The most recent British presidency, held during the first six months of 1998, saw one meeting of EU heads of government in Cardiff in June, and 43 meetings of the Council of Ministers. In addition, the first 'European Conference' was held in London on 12 March 1998. This comprised heads of government from present and potential EU members, except for Turkey which boycotted the meeting because it had been pushed further down the queue of prospective members.

As is usual, the British outlined a series of priorities for their presidency. In the space of just six months the presidency clearly cannot wholly determine the Community's agenda. It must be sensitive to certain key issues as well as the opinions of other member states, particularly that which last held the presidency and that which will hold it next. In effect, there is therefore a troika of the past, current and future presidencies to ensure continuity and coordination. The most important issue facing the British presidency was preparation for EMU and introduction of the single currency. This caused some difficulties because the British government was 'waiting and seeing' and had not committed itself to participation in the euro. Jobs were also a priority for the British government, which expressed a determination to build on the Luxembourg employment summit held in November 1997 and its buzzwords of employability, entrepreneurship, adaptability and equal opportunities. The British also resolved to push forward negotiations on the Agenda 2000 programme with a particular view to securing reform of the funding of agricultural and regional development policies. Finally, enlargement was prioritised. In particular preparations were made for the opening of accession negotiations with Poland, Hungary, the Czech Republic, Estonia, Slovenia and possibly Cyprus in the spring of 1999.

The European Parliament

The European Parliament is the only directly-elected institution at EU level. Direct election means that the most commonly postulated solution to the 'democratic deficit' is more power for the European Parliament because it can make some claim to legitimacy. The Parliament does, though, have problems, one of which is a widespread lack of knowledge of, and interest in, its activities.

Since the accession of Austria, Finland and Sweden in January 1995 there have been 626 members, which, since 1979, have been directly elected. In the 1994-99 Parliament, 542 MEPs were elected by proportional representation and 84 MEPs from the UK by the first-past-the-post system (plus three from Northern Ireland which uses PR). The rest of the UK will fall into line with other EU member states when PR is introduced for the 1999 elections. There are concerns about the number of MEPs rising to unmanageable levels following the accession of central and eastern European countries. At the moment, though, there are fewer MEPs for more than 370 million Europeans than there are MPs for fewer than 60 million Britons.

In the 1980s and 1990s the Parliament has seen its powers strengthened and, emboldened by a sense of democratic legitimacy bestowed by direct election, has tried to flex its muscles in the Union. Direct elections have taken place in 1979, 1984, 1989 and 1994. Turnout levels suggest that European elections have yet to capture the imagination of EU citizens. It tends to be lower for European than for national elections (Table 4.5). This is because European elections are 'second order', that is, they do not change governments and are of less importance than 'first order' national elections. Turnout has been particularly low in Britain where European elections are still essentially domestic contests viewed as an opinion poll on the government and dominated by national issues.

Table 4.5 | **Turnout for elections to the European Parliament, 1979-94 (EU12)**

	Year	Turnout (%)		Year	Turnout (%)
Belgium	1979	91.4	Italy	1979	84.9
	1984	92.2		1984	83.4
	1989	90.7		1989	81.0
	1994	90.7		1994	74.8
Denmark	1979	47.8	Luxembourg	1979	88.9
	1984	52.4		1984	88.8
	1989	46.2		1989	87.4
	1994	52.5		1994	86.6
France	1979	60.7	Netherlands	1979	58.1
	1984	56.7		1984	50.6
	1989	48.7		1989	47.2
	1994	52.7		1994	35.6
Germany	1979	65.7	Portugal	1987	72.4
	1984	56.8		1989	51.2
	1989	62.3		1994	35.6
	1994	60.1	Spain	1987	68.9
Greece	1981	78.6		1989	54.6
	1984	77.2		1994	60.0
	1989	79.9	UK	1979	32.3
	1994	71.2		1984	32.6
Ireland	1979	63.6		1989	36.2
	1984	47.6		1994	36.4
	1989	68.3	EU Total	1979	62.4
	1994	44.0		1984	59.0
				1989	57.2
				1994	58.5

Source F Jacobs, R Corbett and M Shackleton, 'The European Parliament' (Longman, London, 1992), p26; J Lodge, 'The 1994 Elections to the European Parliament' (Pinter, London, 1996), p4

Despite the continued strong national component in European Parliament elections, political parties within the EU are increasingly coalescing in transnational groupings. Article 138A of the Maastricht Treaty noted the important role that transnational political parties can play in the integrative process: 'Political parties at European level are important as a factor for integration within the Union. They contribute to forming a European awareness and to expressing the political will of the citizens of the Union.' After the 1994 elections the Socialists were the largest party grouping in the European Parliament (Table 4.6).

Table 4.6 | **Political groups in the European Parliament, 1998**

Party of European Socialists	215
European People's Party	182
Union for Europe	56
European Liberal, Democrat and Reform Party	43
European Unitary Left	33
Greens in the European Parliament	27
European Radical Alliance	20
Europe of the National States	18
Non-affiliated	32

The 1994 European elections saw Labour, which is a member of the Socialist group, emerge as the largest British party with 62 out of the 87 seats. The Conservatives ranks were decimated with their representation reduced from 32 in 1989 to 18, although such was the abysmal standing of the Conservative Party in the opinion polls at the time that this was seen as not too bad a result. Conservative MEPs are affiliated to the avowedly federalist European People's Party (EPP). The EPP sees itself as an embryonic political party in its own right and has its own federalist programme.

One feature of the European Parliament's deliberations is the number of sites on which they take place: the multi-site problem. The Parliament does most of its work in committees which usually meet in Brussels, although every month for one week, except during August, plenary sessions are held in Strasbourg, while the Secretariat is based in Luxembourg. National interests have prevented a more rational arrangement from being reached. The French spent millions of francs on a new building for the European Parliament in Strasbourg and so did the Belgians in Brussels.

European Parliament powers increased in the 1980s and 1990s. Prior to ratification of the SEA the Parliament had the right to be consulted on legislation. By a two-thirds majority it could vote to sack the Commission and reject the budget. In addition, by the

Treaty of 1970 which established the EC's budgetary framework, the Parliament was made joint budgetary authority, alongside the Council of Ministers. The SEA introduced the cooperation procedure which allowed Parliament a second reading of proposed legislation in specified areas, and the right to suggest non-binding amendments. The SEA also gave the European Parliament power of assent over new members of the Union.

The Maastricht Treaty gave the Parliament powers of co-decision, tilting the balance of power in the Union towards supranationalism. If, within the cooperation procedure, the Council does not approve a Commission proposal then it passes to a 'conciliation committee' on which the Council of Ministers and Parliament are equally represented. They can agree a joint text which must then be approved by QMV in the Council and by simple majority in Parliament. If the conciliation committee cannot agree, then Parliament has the right to reject the Commission's proposal by absolute majority. Co-decision gave the Parliament power of veto in major sectors including single market legislation, consumer protection, health, education and environmental programmes. Maastricht also gave the Parliament power of assent over appointment of the Commission and allowed it to request the Commission to submit a proposal when it decides, by an absolute majority, that new legislation is required.

Amsterdam attempted to simplify decision-making procedures by replacing the cooperation procedure with co-decision and also simplifying the co-decision procedure. This means that areas previously covered by cooperation will be subject to co-decision. The effect of this is likely to be a shift in the balance of power in favour of the Parliament because the conciliation committee will focus on amendments proposed by the European Parliament. Amsterdam also sought to simplify the assent procedure by reducing the cases in which it applies from seven to four (imposition of sanctions for breach of fundamental rights, accession to the EU, uniform electoral procedures, and conclusion of certain international agreements).

The Court of Justice

The shift towards supranationalism in the 1980s and 1990s has placed increased strain on the Court of Justice which has the job of interpreting Community law. The Court, based in Luxembourg, consists of 15 judges, one from each member state, and nine advocates-general. Judges are appointed by agreement of member states for a period of six years, with partial replacement every three years. The advocates-general assist the judges by analysing the arguments of parties in dispute.

As the remit of European integration has expanded so too has the workload of the ECJ. To ease the burden the SEA set up a Court of First Instance which has the power to hear and determine points of law only, with a right of appeal to the Court of Justice. The Court of First Instance is not competent to hear cases brought by member states or Community institutions. The distinguishing feature of Community law is that it overrides national law, this principle being confirmed by the landmark judgment of July 1964 in Costa vs ENEL. In English law it was confirmed in 1974 by Aero Zipp Fasteners vs YKK Fasteners (UK) Ltd. In making the judgment, Mr Justice Graham noted that, 'This [European Communities] Act to put it very shortly enacted that relevant Common Market Law should be applied in this country and should, where there is a conflict, override English law'. Nicoll and Salmon note that:

> The principle is a legal and political milestone and is at the heart of the continuing political controversy over the status of the United Kingdom Parliament, which in the nineteenth century, but not consistently earlier, was held to be 'sovereign' in the sense that its powers were unlimited and incapable of being curbed.[2]

The European Union created by the Maastricht Treaty contained intergovernmental pillars which were separate from the main Treaty and covered sensitive issues of foreign and security policy and justice and home affairs. The Court was excluded from jurisdiction over the work of these pillars. This is why it still makes sense to refer to Community rather than Union law. With certain provisos, the Amsterdam Treaty extends Court competence to free movement, immigration and asylum issues which are taken from the justice and home affairs pillar and gathered together under the heading of the 'area of freedom, justice and security'.

The European Council

The European Council is a meeting of EU heads of government. It was institutionalised in Paris in 1974 and formalised by the SEA in 1986. It meets twice a year (though extra meetings can be held in the event of exceptional circumstances), and convenes in the country holding the presidency of the Union. When Britain held the presidency in the first six months of 1998 the European Council met in Cardiff in June. In addition, a European Conference was convened in March 1998 comprising present and future EU member states.

Article D of the Maastricht Treaty outlined the European Council's role to: 'provide the Union with the necessary impetus for its development and shall define the general political guidelines thereof'. The

European Council served as an important vehicle for the 'preference convergence' that underpinned the resurgence of integration in the 1980s. This can be illustrated by a survey of decisions made at key European Council meetings in the 1980s and 1990s (Table 4.7).

Table 4.7 | **Key European Council meetings, 1984-98**

Fontainebleau (June 1984)	British budget rebate agreed
Milan (June 1985)	Commission's White Paper on completing the single market adopted
London (December 1986)	Doubling of EC regional development funds agreed
Hanover (June 1988)	Delors committee established to examine prospects for economic and monetary union (EMU)
Madrid (June 1989)	Stage One of EMU set to begin on 1 July 1990
Strasbourg (December 1989)	Social Charter agreed; intergovernmental conference (IGC) on EMU established
Dublin (June 1990)	IGC on Political Union agreed
Rome (October 1990)	Stage Two of EMU set begin on 1 January 1994; IGCs on EMU and Political Union opened
Maastricht (December 1991)	Treaty on European Union agreed
Edinburgh (December 1992)	Budget framework to 2000 agreed; 'Cohesion Fund' of Ecu 14.5 billion set up for poorer member states
Corfu (December 1994)	Post-Maastricht IGC launched when 'Reflection Group' on further integration established
Florence (June 1996)	Timetable put in place for lifting ban on export of British beef imposed because of BSE
Amsterdam (June 1997)	Treaty of Amsterdam agreed
Brussels (May 1998)	Eleven participants in third stage of EMU announced.

In the 1980s and 1990s international summitry has been a key feature of world politics. The European variant – the European Council – has been the scene of many landmark decisions in recent Union history. The pace of Union development is strongly influenced by decisions taken by the European Council, which is the pre-eminent political forum within the EU.

A democratic deficit?

The discussion of the components of political integration in Chapter 1 suggested that attitudinal integration should be a characteristic of European political integration as citizens of the European Union begin to identify with the supranational institutions that exercise authority over them. However, perhaps not surprisingly in a Union of more than 370 million people, these institutions can appear distant. This problem of distance is compounded by a relative absence of clear patterns of democratic accountability. One of the central reasons for this is that the EU's political system is an amalgam of both supranational and intergovernmental elements. Neither level is able to exert clear democratic authority over Union activities when common policies have been established.

The most commonly posited solution to the problem of the democratic deficit is increased powers for supranational institutions, particularly the European Parliament. This is seen as capable of bridging the gap between the transfer of competence from national to EU level and the establishment of mechanisms for democratic control. EU institutions are not surprisingly keen advocates of reforms that would increase their own power and influence because they too are players in the game of European integration and not neutral repositories of legal powers. The democratic deficit can actually become a resource for EU institutions because it allows them to make a claim for increased power to close the deficit.

Despite the changes of Amsterdam and Maastricht decision-making authority still resides largely in intergovernmental institutions such as the Council of Ministers and the European Council. Both institutions contain people whose chief responsibilities lie at the national level. National ministers can be reluctant to be held to account at European level. This lack of accountability is reinforced by the fact that the Council of Ministers, unlike legislative authorities in all EU member states, usually meets in secret. Council secrecy results from its combination of legislative and executive roles: it performs the role of both a cabinet and a parliament. Parliaments are very open and usually televised, cabinets are neither. The member states have committed themselves to more 'transparency' for Council deliberations and some sessions of Council meetings have been held in public. Greater openness may mean that on important issues the deals are done outside the formal 'transparent' Council and shift into other secretive bilateral and multilateral forums as member states attempt to safeguard politically-sensitive negotiating positions.

The Commission might also contribute to the democratic deficit because Commissioners are appointed, not elected. The Commission is also very open to organised interests. Due to its small size it relies on the kind of information, expertise and political support which interest groups can provide. Some very close relationships have been forged, such as that between DG VI (Agriculture) and the Committee of Agricultural Organisations (COPA).

Pressure-group activity in Brussels has expanded rapidly and there are now more than 500 'Eurogroups' seeking to exert pressure on EU policy making. Of these about 50 per cent represent industrial interests, 25 per cent the agricultural and food lobbies and 5 per cent are active on behalf of trade unions. Regions are also represented in Brussels. The more powerful regions, such as the German *Länder*, have what are tantamount to embassies in Brussels to ensure that their interests are not neglected. Mitchell argues that 'if one is concerned about the nature of the democratic deficit it is also necessary to be aware of the nature of the relationships which are filling the gap'.[3] In 1998 the European Parliament issued a code of conduct for its members, which covered dealings with lobbyists.

The European Parliament's powers have been increasing, with co-decision-making introduced by the Maastricht Treaty for some policy areas and consolidated by the Amsterdam Treaty. The Parliament has been described as a toothless organisation or a talking shop but its powers exceed those of many national parliaments. Inter-governmentalists, such as the British, fear that a strengthened European Parliament diminishes national parliaments. Many other member states have been keen to see a much greater extension of the European Parliament's powers and argue that democratic structures need to follow the reallocation of powers to the Union level.

It has also been argued that national parliaments and the European Parliament should be partners, not rivals. Where common policies exist then a European Parliament would appear to be the most effective way to scrutinise the activities of politicians and officials who wield power at Union level. Shirley Williams suggests that one way to close the 'democratic deficit' would be to create committees on EU affairs in all member states on which MEPs and national parliamentarians could serve together.[4]

The EU is accumulating an increasingly wide range of powers and responsibilities. If member states wish the Union to reflect the liberal democratic political systems they favour then should not democracy and accountability be the watchwords of builders of the Union? If so, then the technocratic ethos which influenced the creation of the Community in the 1950s, and which still has influence, would need to be confronted. European integration has tended to emphasise efficiency in relation to capital and the market rather than democracy in relation to popular participation and legitimation.

Notes

1 P Ludlow, 'The European Commission', in Keohane and Hoffmann, op cit. ch 3.

2 W Nicoll and T Salmon, *Understanding the European Communities* (Philip Allan, London, 1990), p79.

3 D Mitchell, 'Interest Groups and Democratic Deficit', *Europe Access* 2 (April 1993), pp14-17.

4 S Williams, 'Sovereignty and Accountability in the European Community', in Keohane and Hoffmann, op cit, ch 5.

5 Maastricht and Amsterdam: blueprints for a federal Europe?

The Dutch government has heavily influenced the recent history of European integration. The two EU Treaties signed in the 1990s have both been agreed during a Dutch presidency. For good or ill, the cities of Maastricht and Amsterdam have become closely associated with European integration. The Treaty on European Union was agreed at the Maastricht summit meeting of heads of government in December 1991. As the Treaty staggered through its ratification process, European integration was drawn closer than ever before to the forefront of debate across the continent. Maastricht's centrepiece was a plan for economic and monetary union to be achieved by 1999. The Maastricht Treaty also contained provisions for its own review, which occurred during 1996 and 1997 and resulted in the far less controversial Treaty of Amsterdam, agreed in June 1997. In this chapter, these two Treaties are analysed. Can we detect the outlines of a European federation from them?

Economic and monetary union

The single most contentious issue facing the EU is creation of a single currency. The overarching questions are whether such a European currency union can work and what the implications of such arrangements are for democratic government. Although there is no precedent for a monetary union on such a scale, the historical omens are unclear because as many currency unions have collapsed during the twentieth century as have been created. In Europe, the Belgium-Luxembourg monetary union has survived, but the Austro-Hungarian empire, Czechoslovakia and Yugoslavia all saw political disintegration accompanied by monetary disunion.

The Maastricht Treaty set out a plan for EMU. Despite serious difficulties in the early 1990s, EMU's third stage – transition to a single currency – began on 1 January 1999 with 11 participants, but not Britain. The big question for the British government is whether or not to join the euro early in the twenty-first century. This question will be the subject of a referendum, but the government's recommendation will be crucial. Later, this chapter looks at the Labour government's position on the euro. It believes there to be no major constitutional obstacles to membership, though it recognises that there are economic difficulties associated with convergence with other participating member states. Before analysing Britain's position it is important to survey the recent history of the euro.

Title Two of the Treaty of Rome called for 'progressively approximating the economic policies of member states'. A Monetary Committee was established to seek monetary policy coordination, although there was no clear intention to set up a currency bloc in Europe. The post-war international economic order was centred around the Bretton Woods agreement of 1944 which established the US dollar as the bulwark of the Western economic system.

The basic structures of the Common Market had been set in place by the late 1960s and heads of government, meeting in The Hague in 1969, took steps to form an EMU to protect the CAP. As the setting of common agricultural prices depended on currency stability, instability would threaten its basis. Luxembourg's prime minister, Pierre Werner, was commissioned to bring forward a plan for EMU. He proposed three stages culminating in an irrevocable fixing of exchange rates and free circulation of people, goods, services and capital. However, Werner's plan was undermined by events in the 1970s when dollar instability created by the burgeoning US budget deficit was compounded by the 1973 oil crisis and the failure of EU governments to agree a coordinated economic and political response.

France and Germany relaunch monetary union

The French and German governments remained convinced of the merits of further economic integration. In 1978 the Bremen summit established the European Monetary System (EMS) and its Exchange Rate Mechanism (ERM), with the Ecu as a parallel unit of exchange and forerunner of a single currency. The EMS aimed to formalise economic cooperation between the member states leading to eventual convergence. The Ecu was based on a 'basket' of member state currencies and related to their economic strength. Each national currency was valued in relation to the Ecu and, thus, to all other EU currencies with central rates of exchange.

These Ecu rates of exchange formed the basis of the ERM which sought to establish a zone of currency stability within the EU. The ERM fixed national currencies within narrow margins of fluctuation in relation to the Ecu. In 1978 the margin of fluctuation was set at 2.25 per cent, except for the lira which was allowed to operate within wider margins of 6 per cent. The British joined the EMS in 1979, thus making sterling one of the component currencies of the Ecu. Britain joined the ERM in October 1990 and left rather unceremoniously on 16 September 1992 when sterling was placed under unsustainable pressure on 'Black Wednesday'.

Participating member states, as well as powerful business and industrial interests, saw three main merits in EMU and creation of a single currency:

● It would reduce transaction costs generated by currency exchange
● It would reduce the uncertainty caused by exchange rate fluctuations which undermine the ability of business to plan ahead
● It would coordinate EU economies and thereby help to create the world's most powerful trading bloc.

EMU implies a single currency, coordination of national economic policies with eventual convergence, and mechanisms for inter-regional exchange to compensate poorer economies of the Community. Two political factors have been identified as central to whether or not a currency union can work.[1] Firstly, is there a hegemon that can guarantee stability of the system? One argument advanced for EMU is that it actually reduces the hegemonic power of Germany, although the criteria for EMU are very much German-influenced. Second, is there a sense of community among participating nations? The Maastricht ratification process suggested a gap between political elites and the peoples of Europe that could place pressure on EMU if it fails to deliver prosperity.

EMU also raises constitutional questions. The single market could be passed off as a largely technical measure designed to bring down barriers to trade without great implications for national sovereignty. EMU cannot be passed off in this way. Control of economic policies and the currency go right to the heart of national sovereignty. As Keynes said, 'Whoever controls the currency, controls the government.' Control of key aspects of economic and monetary policy will pass to the Council of Ministers and the European Central Bank in Frankfurt. National sovereignty will be reduced. However, advocates of European integration contend that economic sovereignty is a chimera in the modern era of economic interdependence and that member states can only exercise effective economic sovereignty as part of an economic and monetary union.

Once German reunification became likely in November 1989, the French were keen to hasten movement towards EMU to subsume potential German economic domination in a form of collective economic management. There were however doubts in Germany as many thought the foundations of economic success – an independent Bundesbank committed to price stability – could be put at risk by participation in EMU. The driving forces behind the proposal were Paris and the Commission with support from Italy, Belgium and Spain. Germany's main reason for agreeing to participate was political: commitment to EMU was a way of showing continued faith in European integration. Germany also attempted to ensure that the economic priorities of the EMU plan matched those that had underpinned post-war German economic success. In particular, a commitment to price stability.

The EMU plan In June 1988 the European Council set up a Committee for the Study of Economic and Monetary Union, chaired by Commission President Jacques Delors. Its report, submitted in April 1989, put forward a three-stage plan for EMU.[2] This formed the basis of the timetable agreed at Maastricht.

The three stages on the path to EMU were as follows:

● **Stage One** All countries to enter the ERM. The Madrid summit in June 1989 set 1 July 1990 as the target date for ERM entry. Sterling finally joined on 8 October 1990 with a fluctuation band of 6 per cent around its central rate of DM2.95. Its range was therefore DM3.13 to DM2.77. Market pressure on sterling forced it out of the ERM on 16 September 1992. Pressure on the franc in September 1993 forced a widening of the ERM's bands to 15 per cent
● **Stage Two** By 1 January 1994 all currencies to enter the ERM's narrow band (2.25 per cent). This did not happen because of the ERM crises of 1992 and 1993. A European Monetary Institute was established as the forerunner of a European Central Bank
● **Stage Three** Four convergence criteria were deemed necessary for countries wishing to participate in thia stage of EMU, when a single European currency would be established and an independent European Central Bank set up to run monetary policy. The criteria were:
    Price stability average inflation rate to be within 1.5 per cent of three best performing member states
    Non-excessive government deficits deficits not to exceed 3 per cent of annual GDP; total accumulated government debt not to exceed 60 per cent of GDP
    Stable currency narrow band ERM participation for two years without devaluation
    Low interest rates average long-term nominal rate of interest to be within 2 per cent of that of the three best performing member states.

A deadline of 31 December 1996 was set for the European Council to agree a date for the third stage of EMU. If, by the end of 1997, no date had been agreed then the third stage of EMU would, according to the provisions of the Maastricht Treaty, begin on 1 January 1999. At Maastricht the British and Danes secured opt-outs from this third stage of EMU.

The Maastricht timetable was cast into doubt by the ERM crises of 1992 and 1993. These were caused by the pressures of German reunification. Reunification was extremely costly and generated inflationary pressures in Germany. This pushed up German interest rates and made the Deutschmark strong which, in turn, put other ERM currencies under intense pressure to maintain their ERM parities with the Deutschmark. This was particularly difficult for economies in recession or struggling to emerge from it – such as the British, Spanish and French – that were forced to maintain high interest rates to sustain their ERM membership, even though such policies neglected the needs of their real economies.

Before too long, high interest-rate policies began to lose credibility with financial markets. Speculators eagerly took the opportunity provided by the French referendum of 20 September 1992 to test the resolve of policy makers. On the morning of 16 September a vast amount of money moved out of sterling and into Deutschmarks. The British government refused to countenance devaluation and raised interest rates from 10 to 15 per cent to try to attract dealers back to sterling. The speculative pressure could not be stemmed, and sterling 'floated' out of its ERM band. It was an effective devaluation because rather than floating sterling sank. Ejection from the ERM had deeper political consequences because it shattered the Conservative Party's reputation for economic competence and fuelled dissent within the party over the European issue.

The following week the franc came under sustained pressure and was saved only by heavy Bundesbank backing. However, renewed pressure in July 1993 proved to be irresistible. On 1 August 1993 EC finance ministers gave up the struggle to sustain the ERM. Fluctuation bands were widened to 15 per cent for all participating currencies except the Deutschmark and Dutch guilder. The central purpose of the ERM – exchange rate convergence as part of broader plan for EMU – had been undermined. In 1997, except for the Irish punt which was the weakest ERM currency, all member currencies traded within a spread that never exceeded 4.8 per cent. Despite the ERM's travails the case for a single currency remained strong: 'If sceptics and enthusiasts alike agree on the benefits of the single market, they must also acknowledge the case for stable currencies, however achieved.'[3] Moreover, in addition to the economic case, a powerful political commitment to EMU remained.

The events of 1992 and 1993 made it impossible to proceed to the third stage of EMU in 1997. At the European Council meeting held in Dublin in December 1996 it was decided that there was not a majority of member states fulfilling the necessary conditions for stage three to go ahead and that the EU would not enter the third stage of EMU in 1997. The Amsterdam summit in June 1997 saw member states agree on a growth and stability pact which is designed to ensure budgetary discipline once the third stage of EMU is entered. States which do not meet the requirements of the pact can be fined.

After the delay in 1996 and 1997, the Commission was asked to bring forward further recommendations on progress towards convergence as early as possible in 1998. This it did in a report accepted by the Commission on 25 March 1998. This report was the culmination of a two-year debate about convergence. In Germany there was, and still is, fear that macroeconomic fundamentals that have been closely linked with German economic success will be jeopardised by the euro and countries that have had less rigorous economic management. There was also some creativity in interpretation of the criteria which allowed countries making progress in the direction of attainment to be deemed to have converged. This should not disguise the quite substantial degree of economic convergence that has occurred among participating member states.

At a heads of government meeting held in Brussels on 1-3 May 1998 it was agreed that 11 member states met the criteria. This meant that from 1 January 1999 the exchange rates of the 11 participating currencies were locked and became denominations of the single currency, the euro. The introduction of euro notes and coins will follow three years later on 1 January 2002. National currencies will cease to be legal tender on 1 July 2002 at the latest. The 11 member states that will adopt the euro from 1 January 1999 are: Austria, Belgium, Finland, France, Germany, Ireland, Italy, Luxembourg, the Netherlands, Portugal and Spain. Greece and Sweden did not meet the criteria, while the UK and Denmark had opted-out of stage three. The heads of participating governments appointed Wim Duisenberg from the Netherlands as the first President of the European Central Bank. The eight-year term of office stipulated by Treaty will, however, be split in half to appease the French and allow their candidate, Jean Claude Trichet, to assume the presidency of the bank after four years. It took the meeting 12 minutes to launch the euro and 11 hours to argue who would be the Central Bank's first president.

Britain's position

The UK opt-out only postpones the decision on entry. Would a Labour government recommend a 'Yes' vote in a referendum? On 27 October 1997 in the House of Commons Chancellor Gordon Brown stated that there was not an 'over-riding constitutional bar to membership' and that 'if in the end, a single currency is successful, and the economic case is clear and unambiguous, then the Government believes Britain should be part of it'. This marked a change in tone from the previous Conservative government when Prime Minister Major had been buffeted between the pro- and anti- wings of his fractious party. In opposition, the policy of the Conservatives led by William Hague has hardened to such an extent that they have ruled out membership until 2007 (the lifetime of two Parliaments). Labour seems to be moving in the direction of entry, albeit cautiously, not within the lifetime of the Parliament elected in 1997 and with the additional requirement of a referendum. The Conservatives have established themselves as the anti-euro party.

Chancellor Brown set five economic tests to define whether or not a clear and unambiguous case for membership could be made:

● sustainable convergence between Britain and the euro economies
● sufficient flexibility to cope with economic change
● the effect on investment
● the impact on the UK financial services industry (the City of London)
● the impact on employment.

The House of Commons Treasury select committee was rather critical of the Chancellor's five tests when it noted a certain lack of precision about what is required. As one expert remarked, 'The Chancellor's tests are so loosely defined that anyone will be able to say that they have either been passed or failed according to the dictates of political expediency'.[4] This may be exactly what the Chancellor had in mind because the political controversy surrounding euro membership would make it a risky proposition to bind the government to one position or another.

The first two tests – convergence and flexibility – are central to an economic evaluation of participation in a currency union. Towards the end of 1998, the UK economy was not convergent with those of other EU member states. Base rates in the UK were more than 7 per cent. In France and Germany key official interest rates were just over 3 per cent. There were also major structural differences between the UK and other EU economies which included different trade patterns, a different housing market with higher levels of mortgage debt and Britain's status as an oil-producing nation.

Regarding flexibility, removal of the ability to alter exchange rates leaves two main mechanisms: people moving or wages changing. Both of these are problems for EU member states. Labour mobility within the EU is low, particularly compared to the USA. Real wage change is also quite sluggish. Britain has its own problems with a low skills base, high numbers of workless households and high long-term unemployment. The rest of the EU has problems with high unemployment.

Employment has become a key issue within the EU. Amsterdam added an Employment chapter to the Treaty and greater emphasis was laid on adaptability and flexibility at the November 1997 'jobs summit' held in Luxembourg. One implication of inadequate flexibility could be higher levels of intra-regional transfers – fiscal federalism – within the euro zone from richer to poorer areas. However, with richer member states such as Germany baulking at their level of budget contribution this is far from certain. Without flexibility, however, the euro becomes a risky proposition because if high unemployment remains there may be pressure on the European Central Bank to relax the anti-inflationary policy stance to which it is committed. To avoid inflation and an unravelling of the euro as presently constituted, the quest for flexibility has brought with it pressure for fiscal, welfare and labour market changes.

Another manifestation of flexibility can also be noted in arrangements for the euro: flexible integration. EMU is the first of the Union's major projects to envisage 'ins' and 'outs' (or 'pre-ins'). This was never the case with either the common or single markets. Denmark and the UK are out by choice. Greece and Sweden are pre-in and bound by Treaty to convergence. So too will be the new member states in central, eastern and southern Europe that are likely to join early in the twenty-first century.

The Amsterdam Treaty made no major changes to provisions for the euro because all the important deals had been done at Maastricht. Amsterdam did write flexibility provisions into the Treaty that allow some member states to cooperate more closely and raise the possibility of a two-speed Europe. Before Amsterdam, if a smaller group of member states wished to cooperate more closely a Treaty amendment was required. Amsterdam provides that for pillars I and III of the Treaty closer cooperation can occur if a qualified majority in the Council accepts it and no member state applies a veto.

Britain's stance on the euro, as well as on other issues such as border controls, means that it has remained outside the key integrative measures. It has done this by choice, and can change its decision, though Britain will have been marginal to decision-making on key issues that have important effects if/when it does sign up.

Social policy | There has been a significant change in the attitude of the British government to EU social policy since Labour won the 1997 general election. The Conservative government refused to sign up to post-SEA social policy developments. Other member governments saw enforcement of minimum social standards as a necessary corollary to freedoms given to business by the SEA. At Maastricht Britain secured an opt-out from the agreement on social policy signed by the other 11 member states. In June 1997, Britain moved to opt back into the social policy provisions the Conservatives had opposed.

Even under the Conservatives Britain had not opted-out of EU social policy per se. Britain had already agreed social policy provisions contained in the Treaty of Rome and supplemented by the SEA. These included measures relating to free movement of workers, right of establishment, approximation of laws, health and safety protection, dialogue between management and labour, equal pay for men and women, vocational training and economic and social cohesion.

Development of social policy has been a continuous theme. In 1969 German Chancellor Willy Brandt submitted a memorandum on social policy to The Hague summit arguing that economic integration necessitated social action. In 1972 the Paris summit endorsed the idea of a Social Action Programme which, when launched in 1974, generated attempts to tackle gender inequality. But more ambitious proposals have been blocked. One such was the Vredeling directive on rights of workers to information about their companies.

In 1985 the new Commission President Jacques Delors decided to relaunch the 'social dialogue'. A meeting was held at Val Duchesse, a chateau in the south of Belgium. Pressure for social action came from member states which feared their high standards of social provision could make them uncompetitive in a single market. Once capital can move freely industry may relocate to places where labour is cheap, a process known as 'social dumping'.

The Social Charter | British protests notwithstanding, EU plans for the social domain increased in 1989 when the Commission brought forward its Community Charter on the Fundamental Social Rights of Workers: the Social Charter. The Charter did not have legal effect. It was a 'solemn declaration' signed by 11 member states in Strasbourg in December 1989. Britain refused to sign. The Social Charter outlined rights for workers under 12 headings:[5]

1 Freedom of movement: workers must be allowed to engage in any profession or occupation in the Community
2 Employment and remuneration: all employees must be fairly remunerated
3 Improvement of living and working conditions: each worker has, for example, a right to a weekly paid rest period and paid annual leave
4 Social protection: adequate social protection and social security benefits
5 Freedom of association and collective bargaining: employers and workers have the right of association
6 Vocational training: every worker should have access to vocational training and be able to benefit from further training during his/her working life
7 Equal treatment for men and women
8 Information, consultation and participation of workers: this applies particularly to companies established in more than one member state
9 Health protection and safety at work: satisfactory health and safety conditions in the working environment
10 Protection of children and young people: minimum age of employment not lower than 15, plus limits on the amount of work-time and prohibition of night work
11 Elderly persons: a decent standard of living after retirement
12 Disabled persons: measures to improve social and professional integration.

The Charter crystallised divisions between the British Conservative government and other member states. Prime Minister Thatcher saw in the Social Charter not the moderation of mainstream European Christian Democracy but remnants of Britain's old system of industrial relations with 'beer and sandwiches' for trade union leaders at 10 Downing Street. She was not prepared to invite union leaders in through the front door of Number 10 and was determined that they would not gain entry through a 'back door' opened by Brussels.

The Social Chapter

Prime Minister Major followed his predecessor by opposing any extension of Community social policy. Given the nature of the party he led, there was little room for him to do anything else. Major secured an opt-out from the Social Chapter of the Maastricht Treaty, claiming 'game, set and match for Britain'. The Social Chapter, embodying many rights outlined in the non-binding Social Charter, became an agreement between the other 11 EU member states.

Under Article 2 of Maastricht's Social Chapter the Council of Ministers can issue directives, adopted by QMV, on improvement of the working environment, health and safety, working conditions, information and consultation of workers, equality between men and women and occupational integration. In areas such as social security, redundancy protection and the representation and defence of collective worker and employer interests the Council acts by unanimity. Provisions on pay and the right to strike or impose lockouts were excluded from the Social Chapter. The Amsterdam Treaty extended QMV, although the key issue of social security remained subject to unanimity and pay remained excluded. The replacement of co-operation by the co-decision procedure means greater involvement for the European Parliament over issues such as health and safety, integration of excluded persons, working conditions and treatment of workers. Two directives have been issued using social chapter provisions covering works councils and parental leave.

Amsterdam also added a new Employment chapter to the Treaty. This reinforces the commitment to high levels of unemployment and social protection while reaffirming the importance of competitiveness. A resolution on growth and employment was added to the Treaty. It creates multi-annual employment programmes involving member states and EU institutions.

Britain's opt-out caused some legal difficulties. These came to a head when, in June 1993, the Commission proposed legislation on a maximum 48-hour working week throughout the EU. It did so under Article 118A of the SEA by arguing that long hours could endanger health and safety. Britain had signed the SEA which included Article 118A. The British government challenged the use of this article as the legal basis in the Court of Justice. It argued that a directive on working time was a social chapter matter and therefore did not cover the UK. The Court found in favour of the Commission, making it clear that Britain's opt-out was worth less than first thought.

The decision to opt back in also causes some problems because Britain will not be covered by the social policy provisions until the revised version of EU social policy contained in the Amsterdam Treaty has been ratified. So, for about two years, from the signing of the Treaty in October 1997 until its ratification, transitional arrangements will have to be put in place allowing for UK participation.

Social policy: trouble in store?

Can EU member states maintain their commitment to relatively high levels of social expenditure? In recent years the connections between EMU and social protection have become clear. The quest for economic and monetary union has important implications for social protection in the EU.

Two principal justifications for EU social policy can be advanced:

● **Ideological** Christian Democratic and Social Democratic parties tend to adhere to ideas of 'social solidarity' which seek to build consensus between employers and employees. This conflation of economic and social progress is seen by them as the cornerstone of European economic success in the post-war era and as a necessary condition of future progress

● **Pragmatic** High social costs could lead both to uncompetitiveness and to increased unemployment. However, it is argued that the adoption of minimum standards across the Union could reduce this risk by preventing countries from gaining competitive advantage by lowering their standards of social protection (social dumping).

But a larger question looms which brings into stark focus these ideological and pragmatic considerations and carries with it tough political decisions that could rebound on the EU and support for European integration. Can a 'European social model' be maintained in the face of pressure from economic globalisation and the euro, both of which bring competitiveness into stark focus? Employment and social regulation have become key issues within the EU. The requirement for convergence as part of the transition to the third stage of EMU has imposed macroeconomic disciplines on participating states which have included pressure for reduced government expenditure. This carries political costs because citizens may oppose reduction in valued social protection programmes.

The quest for greater flexibility within a currency union also leads to pressure for changes to existing labour market arrangements and welfare provisions. These were key issues for the Commission's 1993 White Paper on Growth, Employment and Competitiveness and the subject of the 1997 jobs summit in Luxembourg. Indeed, this perspective is at the core of the British Labour government's attitude to EU social policy. Labour's domestic agenda includes commitment to greater labour market flexibility and 'welfare to work'. Both of these domestic priorities, the British government has argued, have a European dimension and would contribute to the EU's 'modernisation' along the same lines as New Labour's plans for Britain.

Citizenship of the Union

Citizenship is closely bound with nationhood. European integration challenges this to some extent by making provision for citizenship of the Union. Under the terms of the Maastricht Treaty all citizens of EU member states also become citizens of the Union. EU citizenship is thus a derived right (from national citizenship). The Treaty does, though, also make it clear that nationality law is a question for the member states and none of the EU's business.

The creation of European citizenship had been advocated since the 1970s because it was seen as one way of closing the democratic deficit. The rights attached to EU citizenship are quite limited and mainly involved a gathering together under the formal heading of EU citizenship of many already-existing provisions or practices. EU citizens have the following rights:

● to move and reside freely within the member states
● to vote and stand as a candidate at municipal and European elections
● to access diplomatic representation from another member state in a country where their own is not represented
● to petition the European Parliament and apply to the European ombudsman in cases of alleged malpractice.

Other aspects of the Treaty in areas such as social policy, employment and free movement, immigration and asylum (all of which were extended by Amsterdam) also touch upon citizens' rights.

One effect of EU citizenship being a derived right is that 'third-country nationals' (people who do not have citizenship of a member state) are not covered by its provisions. There are more than 12 million such people who could be described as the EU's sixteenth member state. Many of these people are permanently resident in EU member states, indeed some are second or even third generation and were born and raised in the EU. They are not, however, citizens of the member state in which they reside because of restrictive laws governing access to national citizenship or because they do not want to renounce the citizenship of their country of origin. Ease of access to the entitlements of European citizenship depends on nationality laws in place in member states.

Maastricht's inter-governmental 'pillars'

The Maastricht Treaty also saw the EU move into areas of high politics, a process continued by the Amsterdam Treaty. However, member states trod cautiously when they decided to incorporate aspects of foreign and security policy and justice and home affairs in the Union. Supranational institutions were peripheral to decision processes in the intergovernmental 'pillars' added by the Maastricht Treaty. The Union created by the Maastricht Treaty with its pillars was likened to a Greek temple. First is the Community 'pillar' within which policies are subject to the involvement of supranational institutions. It makes sense in this Community pillar to talk about Community law because laws that are made have binding effects on member states. Flanking this are two pillars for justice and home affairs, and foreign and security policy. Neither of these pillars created the potential for enactment as supranational laws that were binding on member states. Did this mark the permanent establishment of a new form of intergovernmental cooperation? Or were the pillars temporary measures easing the transition to fuller integration for these contentious policy issues? Amsterdam showed that most member states see the pillars as part of a transition to greater supranationalisation and not as permanent features of the Treaty framework. Britain and Denmark are reluctant to share this vision.

More than 30 years ago it was argued that integration would falter when it had to deal with 'high politics' such as foreign affairs and defence.[6] Member states sought to resolve this problem through intergovernmental cooperation. These provisions were subject to review in 1996. In 1997 the Amsterdam Treaty created an area of freedom, justice and security which moved immigration and asylum from the justice and home affairs pillar into the Community framework.

The common foreign and security policy pillar

In 1970 the member states instigated foreign policy cooperation, known as European Political Cooperation (EPC). EPC attempted to establish an external political profile to match the EC's burgeoning economic power and ensure, where possible, coordination. In 1987 the SEA strengthened EPC by establishing a secretariat to support its operations. The Maastricht Treaty boldly declared in Article J that: 'a common foreign and security policy is hereby established'. In reality the common foreign and security policy (CFSP) pillar was a formalisation of existing EPC procedures rather than a radical new venture, but it does contain some innovations with potential for development.

Within this pillar foreign and security policy has to be decided by a system of 'joint action' with unanimity as the decisional *modus operandi*. However, once 'joint action' has been agreed in principle, majority voting can be used for measures of detail. A decision, say, to send election monitors must be made unanimously, but subsequent decisions about numbers involved and so on can be decided by qualified majority.

These provisions also allow for debate of defence issues previously confined to NATO, EUROGROUP and, from 1984, the revived West European Union (WEU), the European constituent of NATO. In the 1980s the French and Germans were keen to establish a stronger European defence profile. They intensified their own co-operation by setting up the 4000-strong Franco-German brigade, based in Bavaria. Other nations remained wary.

The Maastricht CFSP 'pillar' sought to strengthen the WEU by moving the latter's headquarters, its secretariat, to Brussels, setting up a planning unit, and inviting all non-WEU members of the EU (Denmark, Greece and Ireland) to join. The European Council and Council of Ministers, acting unanimously, were to be central decision-making authorities for both foreign and defence policy. But the differential memberships of the EU and WEU make this difficult: five EU states are only observers in the WEU. NATO is still supreme on the defence side, as the I-FOR operation in Bosnia showed.

War in the former Yugoslavia was a severe test for Community foreign policy. The carnage in Bosnia indicated that the EU failed the test. The USA at first urged Europeans to take the lead in mediating a peaceful solution to a European problem. Yet by 1993 the war's scope and intensity appeared to be beyond the Community's ability to resolve. 'This is the hour of Europe' Luxembourg's foreign minister, Jacques Poos, had proclaimed in June 1991 after brokering another short-lived ceasefire. The Union's failure to resolve a bitter dispute on its doorstep proved a chastening experience. The economic strength of the Union served as a useful asset in peacetime but offered little in the face of bitter ethnic and religious dispute.

Amsterdam added some new provisions to the foreign and security policy pillar. A new post of High Representative was established. This was seen as a way of answering Henry Kissingers's criticism of Europe's lack of a telephone number and weak external profile. The High Representative will be backed by a Policy Planning and Early Warning Unit. The Council is also given power to adopt by unanimity a 'common strategy' to be implemented by joint actions and common positions adopted by QMV, although decisions having military or defence implications will still rely on unanimity. A potential problem is that the appointment of a high-profile High Representative, such as a former head of government or foreign minister, could cause tension between the Union and member states. Amsterdam also strengthened the 'soft security', peacekeeping and humanitarian intervention role of the EU.

The justice and home affairs pillar

The third pillar of the European Union deals with interior policy. Cooperation on internal security issues was actually well-established before Maastricht. The Trevi Group of interior ministers has in fact been meeting since the mid-1970s. In the mid-1980s the SEA gave an impetus to further cooperation by removing internal border checks and thereby heightening the need for cross-border cooperation to tackle issues such as immigration, asylum policy, international crime and drug trafficking.

The Dutch government's original draft of the Maastricht Treaty argued that these policy areas should be incorporated within the supranational structures of the Community. The British government resolutely opposed this, arguing that member states should retain authority over such matters. The third pillar covered issues such as border controls, asylum and immigration policy, combatting drug trafficking, international fraud and cooperation on civil and criminal matters, customs cooperation and matters of common interest. In this pillar decisions are taken on an intergovernmental basis.

On immigration policy EU members are adopting a restrictionist stance with tough border controls. Simultaneously, there is only limited Community action to tackle the problems of racism and neo-fascism that have caused concern in many member states.[7]

The sensitivity of both CFSP and justice and home affairs means that intergovernmental cooperation is preferred to supranationalism and the involvement of Community institutions. One consequence of this is that these policy areas slip into a grey area of democratic accountability between the national and supranational level and thereby reinforce the Community's 'democratic deficit'.

Amsterdam added a new Chapter to the Treaty creating 'an area of freedom, justice and security'. Immigration and asylum were moved from the intergovernmental pillar to this new chapter. Five-year deadlines were imposed for decisions to be reached on many key issues relating to entry, control and residence. The role of the Commission, Court and Parliament is increased, but unanimity in the Council will remain the basis of decision making for at least five years. How unanimity will be reconciled with the five-year deadline for decisions only time will tell, although it is worth noting that when the SEA timetabled a plan for attainment of the single market it also made provision for QMV to facilitate decision making.

Britain chose to opt-out of the new chapter on free movement, immigration and asylum because the implication of the provision is a relaxation of external frontier controls. Both the Conservatives and Labour indicated that they found this passport-control-free Europe unacceptable. Since 1962 Britain has adopted very stringent immigration legislation that has managed to achieve its restrictive targets. Moreover, the abandonment of external frontier controls would imply a shift to internal security checks and the introduction of ID cards, which British people may have difficulty accepting. Ireland also opted-out of the new chapter because it is tied to the UK by a Common Travel Area and participation in the EU's arrangements would have the undesirable effect that Irish citizens would become subject to external frontier controls when travelling between the Irish Republic and Northern Ireland.

Amsterdam also incorporated the Schengen agreement into the Treaty. Schengen deals with free movement issues, immigration and asylum, as well as with 'compensating' internal security measures. The precise location of the Schengen *acquis* – in the new free movement, immigration and asylum chapter, or in the recast justice and home affairs pillar – will be a matter for the Council acting unanimously to decide.

The remainder of the post-Amsterdam justice and home affairs pillar has a much stronger 'drugs and thugs' emphasis on crime prevention, particularly terrorism, trafficking in people, offences against children, illicit drugs and arms trafficking, corruption and fraud. Problems of democratic accountability and judicial review still exist in the third pillar. The heads of governments have resolved to bring the EU closer to its citizens by tackling issues that concern them, such as crime. The chosen fora are highly secretive and may increase the distance between the EU and its citizens. The increased emphasis on internal security in a European single market shows how the distinction between external and internal security has become blurred and how domestic security agencies have had to reorient their role in an increasingly integrated EU to reflect these changes.

Towards a European federation? Can we detect the outline of a European federation from the Maastricht and Amsterdam Treaties? As Chapter 1 showed, the EU already has some signs of federation, such as the distribution of authority between supranational, national and subnational authorities. The steps towards EMU and social policy taken in the Maastricht Treaty consolidate this and if, as looks likely, EMU is attained, signifies a major increase in EU competence. EMU and social protection are closely linked. The convergence and flexibility required by the euro raise tough political questions that have important implications for employment, labour markets and welfare in EU member states. Maastricht also saw a formalisation of co-operation on matters of high politics, which Amsterdam furthered with its creation of a new chapter dealing with free movement, immigration and asylum. External and internal security policies are at the core of national sovereignty, but patterns of cooperation and integration are developing in these areas.

Progress towards deeper integration has not been smooth. The key decisions in European integration require unanimity among member states, and more reluctant ones, like the British, have opposed or opted-out of key aspects of economic and monetary policy, social policy and the planned removal of external frontier controls. One effect of this has been the writing into the Treaty of provision for 'closer cooperation' between more integration-minded member states. This raises the possibility of a two-speed Europe with some kind of 'fast-lane' of Euro-enthusiasts and a 'slow lane' for those either unwilling or unable to match this pace.

The future of Europe may be 'flexible'. It is also likely to be based on the kind of cooperative federalism described in Chapter 2 where member states and the EU share power because none possess the competence or capacity to act decisively on their own. Maastricht and Amsterdam have also helped give the EU a well-nigh impenetrable constitution that is excessively complicated and sometimes defies the understanding of even the most highly trained lawyer. This is usually the result of messy compromises between member states. A simplified constitution for Europe could outline in far more accessible terms key issues such as the rights and duties of EU citizens and mechanisms for control and accountability of EU decision makers.

Notes

1 B. Cohen, *The Geography of Money* (Cornell University Press, Cornell, 1998).
2 Committee for the Study of Economic and Monetary Union, Report on Economic and Monetary Union in the European Community (OOP, Luxembourg, 1989).
3 *Economist*, 7 August 1993.
4 House of Commons Treasury Select Committee, Fifth Report, The UK and Preparations for Stage Three of Economic and Monetary Union, Report HC 503-I (London, HMSO, 1998).
5. European Commission, *Fundamental Charter of the Basic Social Rights of Workers* (OOP, Luxembourg, 1990).
6 Hoffmann, op cit.
7 G Ford, *Fascist Europe* (Pluto Press, London, 1992).

6 Union policies

There is no typical EU policy sector. Each is shaped according to particular circumstances, notably the amount of autonomy member states have been willing to cede by treaty to the Union. Some policy areas are far more supranationalised – controlled by EU institutions than others. In the mid-1970s the Community was basically an institutional mechanism for support of a complicated common agricultural policy that consumed about 80 per cent of the budget. Now the Union has complicated policies designed to promote 'economic and social cohesion'. Taken together, agricultural and cohesion policies consume about 80 per cent of the current budget. This chapter analyses allocation of the Union's budget, the CAP and efforts to create a 'new European agricultural model', and regional development policies and the attempt to create a more 'cohesive' EU.

The budget

In 1998 the EU budget amounted to Ecu 94.4 billion (£63.5 billion). This was 1.26 per cent of total gross national product (GNP) of the 15 member states, and about 2.5 per cent of their combined public spending. By contrast, member states spend about 50 per cent of national GDP. The EU's budget is tiny in relation to that consumed by the central tier in federal systems such as Germany (42 per cent) and the USA (38 per cent).

The EU's budgetary process was created by a 1970 treaty which established three sources of 'own resources'. In 1988 the revenue base of the Union was expanded to take in a fourth own resource. The point about use of the term own resources is that it signifies that the Union is not a club to which members pay a subscription. It has financial independence. The sources of funding are as follows:

- Customs duty levies on imports to member states collected on trade with non-Union countries
- Levies on agricultural trade with non-member countries. These differ from customs duties in that they are not levied at a fixed rate. Instead they fluctuate, and are designed to raise the price of imported agricultural goods relative to those prevailing in the EU
- A proportion of member states' value added tax (VAT) which will decrease to 1 per cent in 1999
- An amount proportional to each member state's share in total Union GNP. This balancing item bridges the gap between EU planned expenditure and own resource yield.[1]

In 1998 the GNP-based own resource constituted 43 per cent of the total budget. The levy on VAT provided 40 per cent in total. Customs duties amounted to 15 per cent of the budget. Agricultural levies were the smallest source at 2 per cent.

Arguments between the Council and Parliament over the budget threatened to derail the Community in the 1980s. In 1980 and 1985 the European Parliament rejected the Commission's proposed budget, and in 1984, 1985 and 1988 the budget had to be topped up by additional national contributions. The financial perspectives agreed in 1988 and 1992 generated a more harmonious relationship between budgetary authorities.

The Council and Parliament share decision-making authority over the budget. This means that the Commission proposes the budget to two joint budgetary authorities. The Council has the final say on what is known as compulsory expenditure, which is that related to the original purposes of the Union as set out in the Treaty of Rome. In the main, this is agricultural expenditure. The European Parliament has the final say on non-compulsory expenditure, which is that spent on areas into which the EU has moved since the founding treaties. In the main, this is regional aid. As the proportion of the budget spent on agriculture declines, and that spent on regions increases, so the authority of the European Parliament expands.

What does the EU spend its money on? The answer is relatively simple: traditionally agriculture, and increasingly the regions. In 1988 an agreement between EU institutions allowed a financial perspective to be developed that took the financial framework through until 1992. At the Edinburgh summit in December 1992 a further agreement extended the financial framework until 1999. Both frameworks sought to control the proportion of the budget spent on s upporting farmers, and to increase the amount of money devoted to less developed regions of the Community. Regional aid – or what are known as EU structural funds – increased from 12.5 per cent to 25 per cent of the Community budget between 1988 and 1992 in a bid to promote what is known in Union parlance as 'economic and social cohesion'. Between 1993 and 1999 the amount spent on cohesion has risen to about 35 per cent of the total budget (Table 6.1).

The EU has been damaged by revelations of fraud and mismanagement. The EU's Court of Auditors uncovered particular abuse of the agricultural budget. This led the Parliament to move a vote of censure on the Commission in January 1999. They were forced to resign in March 1999, and Romano Prodi, the former Italian prime minister, was appointed President. He will serve for the duration of this Commission's term of office and then a full five-year term. The overhaul of the Commission will be the most pressing issue he faces.

Table 6.1 | **Union budget allocations, 1995–99[1]**

	1995	1996	1997	1998	1999
Agriculture	37944	40828	41805	43623	44064
Regions	26329	29131	31477	33461	36618
Internal policies [2]	5060	5337	5603	6003	6231
External policies [3]	4895	5264	5622	6201	6703
Administration	4022	4191	4352	4541	4609
Reserve	1146	1152	1158	1176	1176
Compensation	1547	701	212	99	0
Total	80943	86604	90229	94744	99401

1 1998 prices

2 Expenditure on research and development accounts for between one half and two thirds of this sum

3 The main external policies of the Union are concerned with development aid, agriculture and trade

Source 'Annual Report of the European Union 1997' (OOP, Luxembourg, 1998)

The Commission's Agenda 2000 document envisages that the budget will remain at 1.27 per cent of the Union's GNP until 2006. It argues that the challenges facing the EU can be met from within current spending ceilings, but that this necessitates reform of key policy areas, particularly agricultural policy and regional development, as will be seen below.

Agriculture | Initially, the Common Agricultural Policy was seen as an EU success, as its establishment in 1962 and phased introduction by 1968 marked the establishment of a supranational decision-making process in an important area of economic activity. However, the policy became a by-word for wastefulness. There has been strong internal pressure for reform because the CAP led to over-production and the creation of butter mountains, wine lakes and the like. External pressures have been exerted by the liberalisation of world trade which rendered the protectionist CAP unsustainable. The expenditure implications resulting from the accession of new member states in central, eastern and southern Europe with relatively large agricultural sectors are also potentially serious. Since 1992 reforms of the CAP have attempted to deal with this wastefulness and reorientate the CAP. The proportion of the EU budget spent on agriculture is currently declining. By the end of this century it will have fallen to 45 per cent from the 80 per cent registered at the end of the 1970s. The reform process is ongoing.

Article 39 of the Treaty of Rome outlined five objectives for the CAP: to increase agricultural productivity; to ensure a fair standard of living for the agricultural community; to stabilise markets; to assure the availability of supplies; and to ensure reasonable prices to consumers. These objectives were to be attained by institution of common prices for agricultural produce within the Community. Prices are decided annually by the Council of Ministers in the first half of the year, on the basis of proposals made by DG VI of the Commission. The weakness of this system was that prices tended to be set too high. By presenting farmers with a relatively inelastic demand curve, this stimulated over-production with the effect that agricultural surpluses built-up.

One reason for high price levels was the political power of farmers. Agricultural interest groups are influential at both domestic and supranational level. COPA has about 50 full-time staff in Brussels. These are supplemented by full-time officials of national associations, of which the British National Farmers' Union (NFU) has between five and 10. The activities of agricultural lobby groups are not countered by groups of commensurate strength representing consumer or environmental interests, and have been very influential.

The CAP developed a reputation for wastefulness, high prices and protection of farmers' interests. There were also serious problems of environmental damage because of incentives for intensive production. Typically, large-scale farmers have profited from the system at the expense of consumers who must pay higher prices. It has been argued that the CAP is a victim of its own success as it set out to try to increase productivity and promote self-sufficiency and has done so, admittedly at the cost of high prices and surpluses.[2] Perhaps this view is overly charitable: if the CAP represented success, then failure would be a sight to behold. In the 1980s and 1990s the Commission embarked on a programme of reforms.

It was the expense of the CAP that generated pressure for reform. In the 1980s the British, Dutch and Danish governments were instrumental in pushing for improvement of the system as they had small and relatively efficient agricultural sectors which gained little from the policy (Table 6.2). The impetus for reform was strengthened by the accession of Greece, Portugal and Spain in the 1980s, all of which have relatively large agricultural sectors which placed additional strain on the CAP.

A series of reforms was introduced in the 1980s. In 1984 milk quotas were initiated to reduce over-production. In 1985 an effective price cut for agricultural produce was agreed when the price package provided for an increase of 1.8 per cent compared with an inflation rate of 5.8 per cent. In 1986 the price increase was 2.2 per cent while inflation was 2.5 per cent. In 1987 a price freeze was introduced for cereals and vegetables.

Table 6.2

Agricultural efficiency of EC member states, 1991[1]

Country	% Employment	% GDP	Ratio
Netherlands	4.5	4.0	89
Belgium	2.7	2.1	78
UK	2.2	1.4	71
Luxembourg	3.1	2.2	71
Ireland	13.8	9.5	69
Denmark	5.5	3.7	67
Greece	21.6	13.9	64
France	5.8	3.3	57
FRG	3.3	1.5	45
Spain	10.7	4.6	43
Italy	8.5	3.6	42
Portugal	17.5	5.3	30
EC12	6.2	2.9	47

1 Agricultural 'efficiency' is calculated by dividing GDP devoted to agriculture by percentage employment in agriculture, and by multiplying by 100

Source 'European Community Bulletin of the European Communities 1993'

In the light of the 1988 budget agreement a further series of reforms was agreed:

● **Stabilisers** Production over limits led to price cuts, thereby making it uneconomic to expand production
● **Set-aside** Farmers were subsidised to take land out of production
● **Co-responsibility levies** Ostensibly to assist product marketing, in reality the levy was a tax on production.

In 1993 the Commission reported that the impact of reform had been minimal as surplus stocks had continued to rise. 'The reforms of the years 1985-88 have not been implemented and are themselves incomplete. It is not surprising that under these conditions the CAP finds itself once again confronted with a serious crisis.'[3] The system of price guarantees led to over-production. Consequently surpluses grew while the in-built incentive to intensive methods of production caused environmental damage. The Community found itself paying more and more money to large-scale producers while generating no solution to general problems of low farm incomes.

A further package of reforms was agreed in 1992 and introduced in 1993. These sought to move away from a price-support policy to direct aid for producers in a bid to reduce over-production and establish a closer relation between EU and world prices. The principal measures were:

- Over three years a major reduction of 29 per cent in cereal prices and 15 per cent in beef
- More effective measures to manage supply, such as set-aside arrangements for arable land
- Introduction of a system of permanent compensatory aid to neutralise the negative effects on income caused by the decision to reduce prices for cereals, oil seeds and beef
- Development of an agri-environmental action programme to encourage farmers to adopt less polluting and more environmentally-sensitive methods of production
- Financial incentives for farmers who agree to whole or partial afforestation of their land
- An early retirement scheme for farmers aged 55 or above.

There were also external pressures for reform of the CAP. The 1992 reforms allowed the EU to comply with its obligations under the Uruguay round of the world trade talks and associated pressure for liberalisation of world trade. This required a 20 per cent reduction in domestic support for agriculture over a five-year period, a 36 per cent reduction in spending on export subsidies, and a 21 per cent cut in the quantity of subsidised exports.

The Commission's Agenda 2000 document recognises the connection between reform of the CAP and management of the Union's finances. This has become particularly important because of potential future strains on the budget caused by new member states in central, eastern and southern Europe with relatively large and efficient agricultural sectors. Agenda 2000 calls for a deepening of the 1992 reforms in response to three main challenges. Firstly, price levels are still too high for the EU to take advantage of the expansion of world markets. High prices lead to a familiar scenario: stocks start to build up and push up budget costs. Second, despite some success the negative effects of the CAP were only partially corrected by the 1992 reforms. In particular, the support provided was distributed unequally and concentrated on regions and producers which were not among the most disadvantaged. This had negative effects on regional development. Third, the development of excessively intensive farming practices has not been checked, with the result that they continue to have a serious impact on the environment and animal diseases. A 1998 report by the UK Countryside Commission showed that in some cases the changes actually did more harm than good by encouraging farmers to plough up meadows to plant potatoes or other heavily-subsidised crops such as flax. The report argued that the reforms had 'failed to encourage farmers to switch to more sustainable farming practices'.

In its evaluation of the reforms the Commission called for a new decentralised model which would give member states the ability to settle issues for themselves by taking better account of a given sector or set of local conditions. It did, however, warn that this should not go so far as to renationalise agricultural policies. Among the Commission proposals presented in March 1998 were:

- price cuts
- increased direct aid with an increased national level component to reflect local circumstances better
- simplification of the rules
- the reinforcement of action on the environment with current aid linked to less intensive farming methods
- rural development to become a second pillar of the CAP, backed by EU funding for development schemes across all rural areas.

These kinds of measures, the Commission hopes, will create a new European model of agriculture that according to the Commission wish-list is competitive, environmentally friendly, able to supply quality products while maintaining the visual amenity of the countryside and generating and maintaining employment. This implies a rejection of the failings of the old CAP.

Regional policy

The Treaty of Rome contained no specific commitment to regional policy, apart from a generalised concern to secure 'balanced economic expansion'. Pressure from Italy and Ireland led to creation of the European Regional Development Fund (ERDF) in 1975, with a budget of £540 million. The budget was doubled in 1977. However, increases in inflation and the severe impact of economic recession meant that this increase did not represent a real advance. Pressure for expanded regional aid grew in the 1980s when Greece, Portugal and Spain entered the Community. In some ways increases in regional aid were a 'side payment' made to poorer states to secure their agreement to the single market.[5] A consequence of the development of Treaty competence to deal with regional inequalities is that the role of supranational institutions has expanded. In particular, the Commission has been at the forefront in promoting the Europeanisation of regional policy.

There are marked regional disparities between and within EU member states. The poorest member states are Greece, Spain and Portugal. Other parts of the Union also lag behind, such as southern Italy, parts of the UK, eastern Germany (what was the GDR) and southern Spain. If average EU gross domestic product (GDP) is set at 100, then average GDP in 1997 in Portugal was 47.7, in Greece it was 51.8 and in Spain 64.9. About 25 per cent of the EU's population live in regions in which GDP per capita is 25 per cent below the EU average. Disparities can be marked within countries. In the UK Northern Ireland, Merseyside and the Scottish Highlands and Islands all qualify for high levels of regional aid as what are known as 'Objective One' areas.

At the time of the SEA the poorer member states were concerned that their infrastructural and skills bases were not sufficiently developed to allow them to compete effectively in the single market. The SEA added a new Title V on 'Economic and Social Cohesion'. The Maastricht Treaty charged the heads of government with establishing a Cohesion Fund to supplement the development effort within the Community. The fund was established at the Edinburgh summit in December 1992. Member states whose GNP was below 90 per cent of the Community average were eligible for assistance. This generated four 'cohesion countries': Greece, Ireland, Portugal and Spain. The Cohesion Fund provides financial support up to 80-85 per cent for environment or transport infrastructure projects.

Three main sources of regional aid are now available through EU structural funds:

● **European Regional Development Fund** (ERDF) The largest of the four structural funds. It consumes about 50 per cent of the total structural funds budget and is particularly targeted on infrastructural development in poorer regions
● **European Agricultural Guidance and Guarantee Fund** (EAGGF) Divided into two sections: the Guarantee Section finances price-support measures for farmers; and the Guidance Section subsidises rationalisation schemes, modernisation and structural improvements
● **European Social Fund** (ESF) Funds vocational training, retraining and job-creation schemes targeted particularly at unemployed youth, the long-term unemployed, socially disadvantaged groups and women.

In the late 1990s there were seven criteria by which regions could qualify for assistance from the EU. The Commission has introduced a subjective element into structural fund allocations. Instead of relying entirely on sets of 'objective' figures – levels of GDP, unemployment and so on – it encourages regions to make a case for receipt of assistance. The fact that this case must be made at the regional level evidently poses problems within England, which has no elected regional tier of government. It has prompted both private- and public-sector institutions to seek enhanced regional coordination. The North West Partnership, for example, brings together groups such as the North West Regional Association, the North West CBI and TUC and the North West Business Leadership Team, plus chambers of commerce, local universities and members of the voluntary sector. The Partnership attempts to present a united front for the region on regional development policy at national and European level. The seven criteria for award of EU funds are:

● **Objective One** Promotion of regions lagging behind, in particular those with a GDP per capita of less than 75 per cent of the Community average during the previous three years, as well as regions with GDP around that mark and for which there are special reasons for inclusion. About 25 per cent of EU citizens (92.1 million people) live in Objective One regions. In the UK, 6 per cent live in the three eligible regions: Northern Ireland, Merseyside and the Scottish Highlands and Islands
● **Objective Two** The three main criteria are: an unemployment rate above the Community average; a percentage share of industrial employment higher than the Community average; a decline in this employment category
● **Objective Three** Reduction of long-term unemployment and integration into working life of the young and of persons excluded from the labour market; promotion of equality for men and women in the labour market
● **Objective Four** Facilitating the adaptation of workers to industrial change and to changes in productions systems
● **Objective 5a** Promotion of rural development by speeding up adjustment of agricultural and fishing industry structures
● **Objective 5b** Areas with a low level of socio-economic development and a high share of agricultural employment, a low level of agricultural income and low population density and/or depopulation. The biggest beneficiaries are Austria, Finland and France
● **Objective Six** Areas with a very low population density. Applies to parts of Sweden and Finland.

The Agenda 2000 programme proposes a reduction in the number of Objectives from seven to three. By 2006 it is estimated that recast Objectives One and Two will cover between 35 and 40 per cent of the Union's population. Both will have a regional focus. Objective One will continue to cover areas where GDP is less than 75 per cent of the EU average. Objective Two will cover areas affected by changes in the industrial, service or fisheries sector, rural areas in serious decline and urban districts with serious difficulties. A new Objective Three will have a human-resources focus and be devoted to helping member states adapt and modernise education, training and employment.

By means of its developing regional policy the Commission is slowly building a network of regional partners. Countries with already-established regional authorities tend to have better contacts. The Maastricht Treaty also established a Committee of the Regions in an attempt to get subnational input into EU decision-making. Maastricht requires consultation with the Committee on trans-European networks, public health, education, youth, culture and economic and social cohesion. One result of this kind of activity is that the Commission and European regions establish links that by-pass member states. That said, the Committee of the Regions is strictly a consultative body and has no legislative authority. Member-state agreement is necessary before anything substantive can be made of these contacts. This means that national governments remain key gatekeepers on the European scene. Nevertheless, it is increasingly possible to talk meaningfully of an emergent 'Europe of the regions', particularly within member states that have an established regional tier.

The Union in action

As was noted at the start of this book, EU and domestic politics are becoming increasingly entwined in member states. In Britain this is happening in a wide range of policy areas. Three areas are surveyed here. They are pensions, privatisation and the BSE crisis.

In the sphere of pensions, a 1989 ECJ decision (Barber vs Guardian Royal Exchange) means that equal retirement ages for men and women now have to be phased in across the Union. Currently, women in Britain retire at 60 and men at 65. In 1980 Barber argued before an industrial tribunal for equal treatment between the sexes in the pensions sphere. The ECJ cited Article 119 of the Treaty of Rome – which provides for equal pay for men and women – in upholding his claim. The decision in the Barber case was a legal landmark because it acknowledged that occupational pension schemes count as pay. It obliged the British government to set in train legal changes which will equalise retirement ages at 60. The cost will be enormous: pension funds estimate it at up to £2 billion per annum. In future years, as the pressure of an ageing society is felt, there are likely to substantial problems in finding this extra money. Unfortunately the wheels of European justice turn slowly and the man who brought the case, Douglas Barber, a claims manager for GRE in Sheffield, died in 1989 before the ECJ decision was reached.

The British privatisation drive was one of Thatcherism's flagship policies. It too was affected by EU law. A 1977 EC directive on acquired rights for workers was incorporated into British law as the Transfer of Undertakings (Protection of Employment) (TUPE) regulation in 1981. This lays down that when an operation is privatised employees transfer to the new undertaking their original rights and conditions of employment. Redundancies can be treated as unfair dismissals. In July 1993, 18 sacked refuse collectors in Hastings won an historic legal victory when the Employment Appeals Tribunal in London upheld their claim that their dismissal after local refuse services had been privatised contravened TUPE. Councils and other public-sector employers, such as health authorities, could now face thousands of claims from workers who have lost their jobs or had inferior pay and conditions imposed as a result of contracting-out.

Agricultural policy is one of the most supranationalised policy sectors. The power of EU institutions over the British agricultural industry was made very clear in March 1996, following the announcement of a possible link between a cattle disease, Bovine Spongiform Encephalopathy (BSE) and its human equivalent Creutzfeldt-Jakob Disease (CJD). The Commission imposed a complete ban on the export of UK cattle and beef products such as gelatine, tallow and semen. The British government took the Commission to the Court of Justice, but in May 1996 the Court upheld the Commission's ban. The Florence European Council of June 1996 put in place a timetable for lifting the ban, including the slaughter of an estimated 85,000 animals aged more than 30 months and deemed to be at risk because of their association with infected cattle. The effects on the UK beef industry have been substantial. In 1995 Britain exported beef worth £594 million and live calves (another controversial issue because of the animal-rights implications of transporting live animals) worth £73 million. It is reported that between 1996 and 1998 1000 jobs were lost and that the ban had cost £1.5 billion, including government eradication measures. In June 1998 the Commission recommended that the export ban be lifted for de-boned beef from cattle aged six to 30 months born after 1 August 1996. Exports from Northern Ireland had been allowed to recommence from 1 June 1998, reflecting the isolation of that industry from mainland Britain. The Commission's recommendation for a more general relaxation of the ban received a cool response from the EU's Standing Veterinary Committee and it was touch and go whether the Council would lift the ban by the autumn of 1998, although it did. The costs of the ban continue to mount while a government established committee of inquiry probes the origins of the crisis.

A change of emphasis

The Union's main concern continues to be agricultural policy, but pressure for reform has led to a policy reorientation including a switch from price to income support. The amount of money spent on agriculture is declining both as a proportion of the budget and in real terms. Increasingly, EU money is spent on poor regions of the Union (some of which are agricultural). This movement towards an emphasis on economic and social cohesion represents a shift away from the original market-based purposes of the Union and an increased emphasis on a social dimension. The EU now seeks a wider responsibility for the living standards of its citizens.

When the EU acquires powers for particular policy sectors then supranational institutions have increased scope to affect the lives of EU citizens in areas such as pensions, employment law and agricultural policy. The snapshots of Union action presented at the end of this chapter give some insight into the ways in which Britain is obliged to yield to EU law in areas where it has agreed to pool sovereignty. This may generate some tension with domestic political priorities, but EU law has direct effect and overrides national law where they conflict. This emergent policy dimension above the nation state means that there are significant and developing supranational (as well as subnational) dimensions to European politics.

Notes

1 This fourth source of funds is linked to the relative wealth of members, meaning that the rich pay more and that a redistributive element enters the Community's funding arrangements.
2 M Holland, *European Community Integration* (Pinter, London, 1993).
3 European Commission, 'The Development and Future of the CAP', *Bulletin of the European Communities*, Supplement 5/91 (OOP, Luxembourg, 1991), p11.

7 A wider and deeper community

Can a wider EU with more members be a deeper EU with closer economic and political integration? This is a key question for the Union as it confronts the likelihood that there will be perhaps 25 or 30 member states by early in the twenty-first century. Will this increase in membership dissipate the integrative impetus or will it harden commitment to deeper integration? In the past it has been seen as essential that deepening accompany widening. In 1973 Britain, Denmark and Ireland entered, followed by Greece in 1981 and Spain and Portugal in 1986. In 1995 the 12 became 15 when Austria, Finland and Sweden joined. Over much the same period the Union has 'deepened' as a result of the SEA, the Maastricht Treaty and the Amsterdam Treaty. By the end of the 1990s a queue of countries in central, eastern and southern Europe was lining up for membership.

A wider community

Article O of the Maastricht Treaty states that 'Any European State may apply to become a Member of the Union. It shall address its application to the Council, which shall act unanimously after consulting the Commission and receiving the assent of the European Parliament, which shall act by an absolute majority of its component members.' The term 'European' has not been officially defined, but is seen as combining geographical, historical and cultural elements which all contribute to the European identity but cannot be condensed into a simple formula.

The 1998 'Accession Partnerships', agreed with 10 central and eastern European states, outline three general principles of membership:

● stability of democratic institutions, respect for the rule of law, human rights and respect for minority rights. For instance, before it joins Bulgaria is, among other things, expected to adopt legislative provisions on minority language use
● a functioning market economy and the ability to cope with competitive pressures and market forces. Poland, for instance, is required under the terms of its Accession Partnership to restructure its steel industry
● an ability to accept the obligations of membership. Applicants are expected to adopt the necessary legislation for participation in the single market, to meet the requirements of economic convergence and to put in place tough immigration and asylum policies. There are no 'opt-ins' or 'opt-outs' available for applicant member states, although

the possibility of flexible integration has certainly been created by the Amsterdam Treaty.[1]

Meanwhile, existing member states, linked with the Agenda 2000 programme, are seeking to restructure agricultural and regional policies to put in place a financial framework for the Union capable of dealing with new accessions. This prompts a disguised criterion: that new accessions should not have severe budgetary implications.

EFTA and the EEA

Despite being established as an alternative model of European cooperation rather than integration, the European Free Trade Association (EFTA) has seen many of its member states join the EU. In April 1984 the Luxembourg Declaration by EC and EFTA ministers expressed a desire for extended cooperation, in particular through free-trade agreements. This declaration was consolidated in Oporto in 1991, when the European Economic Area (EEA) was agreed. This was not formalised until May 1992, when a dispute with the ECJ over legal jurisdiction had been resolved. The EEA came into effect in 1993. It extended free movement of people, goods, services and capital to the seven members of EFTA and thereby created a single market of more than 380 million people. The EEA document is fatter than the Treaty of Rome, weighing in at 100kg. It contains 15,000 pieces of legislation which EFTA countries must incorporate into their legal systems. Although the EEA is designed to maximise trading benefits, some EFTA countries are displeased that they must abide by EEA laws but are only allowed a consultative role in shaping them. The EEA also served as a halfway house to Union membership for Austria, Sweden and Finland.

The 1995 accessions had some interesting implications for new member states. Austria, Finland and Sweden were obliged to reconsider their neutrality in the light of the requirement to accept the common foreign and security policy as part of the EU's *acquis*. The end of the Cold War allowed the three new members to redefine their defence and foreign policy identity in a European context. The Swedish government, for instance, referred to 'Swedish foreign and security policy with a European identity'.[2]

Even though Norway is a member of NATO and did not have the security policy problems of Finland and Sweden, its people opposed EU membership. Reasons for this include the country's status as an oil-producing nation, and fears of the impact of accession on its agricultural and fishing industries. With Britain, Norway made application bids which were rejected in 1963 and 1967. Again with

Britain, a reapplication in 1970 was accepted and a treaty of accession signed in 1972. However, in a referendum in September 1972 the Norwegian people rejected membership: 53 per cent voted 'No'. Subsequently Norway's trade links with the Union have continued to intensify: by 1990 nearly 60 per cent of its trade was with the EU. In 1994, the Norwegian people again rejected EU membership.

The prospect of membership of a supranational organisation seems to hold little appeal to the Swiss people, who narrowly voted to reject membership of the EEA in a December 1992 referendum: 51 per cent were against, 49 per cent in favour. A remarkable aspect of this episode was not that the Swiss voted 'No', but that a country that does not even have a domestic single market should have applied for EU membership in the first place. In December 1992 a referendum in Liechtenstein approved membership of the EEA. Iceland has also joined the EEA but has ruled out an application for EU membership in the near future.

Expansion in central and eastern Europe

In the years ahead the EU's geographical axis will tilt eastwards as countries in central and eastern Europe join the EU. Accession of former Soviet-bloc countries presents more problems for the Community than membership of EFTA/EEA countries. This is primarily because of their economic profiles of the two groups.

In the aftermath of the Cold War, the G7 summit in Paris in October 1989 asked the Commission to coordinate a planned programme of economic aid for Poland and Hungary, called PHARE. Other OECD member states supported this initiative and came together to form the G24 (12 EU member states, six EFTA countries, the USA, Canada, Japan, New Zealand, Australia and Turkey). In July 1990 the G24 agreed to extend the programme to the former GDR, the Czech Republic, Slovakia, Bulgaria and what was then Yugoslavia. The PHARE programme had five priorities: access to donor countries' markets for goods produced by beneficiaries; development of agricultural and food industries; investment promotion; training; and environmental protection.

In the late 1990s the PHARE programme was reoriented to prepare recipient countries for EU membership. One effect of this is that from 1998 onwards about 30 per cent of PHARE assistance (Ecu 6700 million between 1995 and 1999) will be directed towards institution building, including the strengthening of democratic institutions. The other 70 per cent will be directed towards infrastructure development, such as agricultural restructuring and regional policy.

In preparing them for eventual membership, the EU has sought
closer links with central and eastern European countries. To begin
with Europe Agreements were concluded with Poland, Hungary, the
Czech Republic, Slovakia, Bulgaria, Romania, Estonia, Latvia and
Lithuania and Slovenia. The preamble to the agreements makes the
eventual intent quite clear: 'Having in mind that the final objective
of [Poland/Hungary/Slovakia/etc] is to become a member of the
Community and that this association... will help to establish this
objective.' The main areas covered by the Europe Agreements were
political dialogue, free trade and freedom of movement, economic
cooperation, financial cooperation and cultural cooperation.

The Agenda 2000 document sought a more focused pre-accession
strategy by bringing pre-accession support within one 'Accession
Partnership' document with the 10 signatory states of the Europe
Agreements. In Agenda 2000 the Commission noted that:

> The reinforced pre-accession strategy has two main objectives.
> First, to bring together the different forms of support provided
> by the Union within a single framework, the Accession
> Partnerships, and to work together with the applicants, within
> this framework, on the basis of a clearly defined programme to
> prepare for membership, involving commitments by the
> applicants to particular priorities and to a calendar for carrying
> them out. Secondly, to familiarise the applicants with Union
> policies and procedures through the possibility of their
> participation in Community programmes.[3]

By early in the twenty-first century it is possible that 10 central and
eastern European countries will have satisfied the terms of their
Accession Partnerships. The Commission's Agenda 2000 document
stated that negotiations should be opened as soon as possible with
Hungary, Poland, Estonia, the Czech Republic and Slovenia.

**Southern
enlargement**

The third group of countries to seek EU membership are on its
southern flank: Turkey and Cyprus. In July 1987 Morocco applied
for membership but was not considered to be a European country
and the application was rejected.

Turkish and Cypriot accession have caused considerable difficulties
for the EU. The Turks applied in 1959. A 1963 association agreement laid out a three-stage timetable for accession that should have
seen Turkey admitted in 1995. In December 1995 a customs union
entered into force; but Turkey remains outside the EU and prospects
for accession have diminished as central and eastern European

accessions have been prioritised. In November 1997 the Turkish foreign minister said that Turkey would drop EU membership from its political agenda if the EU did not see Turkey as a potential member. The December European Council meeting failed to list Turkey as a prospective member state. In March 1998 the Turkish government boycotted the inaugural European Conference held in London with 26 existing and prospective member states. This conference was largely designed to assuage Turkish concerns about future accession, but as Foreign Minister Ismail Cem noted: 'It would be meaningless for Turkey to be present at a conference that will have no meaning, no essence, especially if Turkey is not going to be a candidate'.

When the June 1998 Cardiff summit meeting of EU heads of government failed to put Turkey on an equal footing with other candidate countries, such as its neighbour Bulgaria, the Turkish government 'froze' relations with the EU. Germany and Luxembourg joined Greece in opposing release of a statement suggesting that Turkey was at the same stage in the process as other applicant states. A concern for other more sympathetic member states, and for the USA, was that Turkey would turn its attention eastwards with balance of power implications between the west and Muslim nations.

A sub-text may be that Turkish accession would bring a Muslim country into the EU, while its position straddling Europe and Asia has generated doubts about whether or not Turkey can claim to be a European country. The leader of the German Christian Democratic parliamentary party clearly thought not when he was reported as remarking in January 1995 that Turkey was not a European country and that 'All the prime ministers who pretend to be favourable to Turkish accession are hypocrites'. Turkish accession would also have economic implications, although no more serious than those posed by some of the poorer eastern European countries. Turkish GDP per capita stood at $2700 in 1997, while 15 per cent of national income was derived from the agricultural sector.

A main cause of tension between Greece and Turkey is the status of the divided island of Cyprus. While the island remains divided Cypriot accession is problematic. Tensions over Cyprus and Turkey overshadowed the European Conference. Greece threatened to block the EU's eastward enlargement if the Turks were allowed a veto over the accession of Cyprus. The EU also wanted Turkish northern Cyprus to be represented on the Cypriot negotiating team, but the Turkish Cypriots refused to participate. At the London meeting in March 1998 Tony Blair argued that the EU should push ahead with talks, but French President Jacques Chirac cautioned that: 'If Cyprus has a vocation to join the EU, the Union does not have a vocation to take in only a piece of Cyprus and integrate conflicts that are not its own'. The deployment of Russian SS-300 missiles by the Greek Cypriots in 1997 and 1998 heightened tension in the area.

Deepening of the Community

The question of future widening has raised the salience of deepening economic and political integration. This is typically seen as involving both policy and institutions. It is clear that new accessions will place additional strain on both the institutional and policy structures of the Union. There are policy ramifications that necessitate regional policy and agricultural policy changes within a revised budget framework. Former EFTA/EEA countries were largely compatible with other Union members. This may not be the case to the same extent for central and eastern European countries. A comparison with southern European accessions in 1981 and 1986 may be more appropriate. Further widening of the Union may lead to pressure for deepening of integration to ensure that the Union is not weakened by enlargement. In 1992 the Commission noted the need for deepening to accompany widening: 'Non-members apply to join because the Community is attractive; the Community is attractive because it is seen to be effective; to proceed to enlargement in a way that reduces its effectiveness would be an error'.[4]

Institutional deepening involves strengthening the Union's supranational structures. Despite impending new accessions, the Amsterdam Treaty was seen as fudging the difficult issues associated with institutional reform. A protocol attached to the Treaty provides that a 'constitutional conference' be held at least one year before membership of the Union exceeds 20. It also provides that on the date of the first enlargement the Commission will comprise one national for each member state (currently the five largest member states have two Commissioners). This will only happen if there has been a readjustment of voting procedures in the Council to compensate the larger countries. It takes the optimistic view that the Union's institutions could continue to function satisfactorily with five new member states.

Notes

1 The full texts of all the Accession Partnerships can be found at:
http://europa.eu.int/comm/dg1a/enlarge/access_partnership/index.htm
2 European Commission, 'Europe and the Challenge of Enlargement: Commission Opinion on Sweden's Application for Membership', *Bulletin of the European Communities*, Supplement 5/92 (OOP, Luxembourg, 1992).
3 European Commission, *Agenda 2000 Volume 1*, Doc. 97/6 (OOPEU, Luxembourg, 1997).
4 European Commission, 'Europe and the Challenge of Enlargement', *Bulletin of the European Communities*, Supplement 3/92 (OOP, Luxembourg, 1992), p14.

8 British membership assessed

The impact of European integration on British politics was particularly important between 1992 and 1997 when the Maastricht Treaty and the tortuous ratification process split the Conservative Party. Chapter 3 investigated the EU policy of successive British governments. This chapter brings the analysis together by examining the impact of European integration on contemporary British politics and the 'Europeanisation' of British economic and political life occasioned by EU membership. The formal dimension of this change is incorporation of EU law into British law. Informally, the process of integration manifests itself in an array of economic, political, cultural and social linkages. There is strong evidence that the British economy is closely connected with those of its European partners. Politically and socially evidence of integration is less great.

Economic impact of membership

The main feature of the Community Britain joined in 1973 was the customs union established by the Treaty of Rome and the linked aspiration to create a single market. Intensified links with the EU have altered British trade patterns, which are now predominantly focused on the continent of Europe. In 1958 21 per cent of UK exports went to EC member states; by 1994 this had risen to 54 per cent. Over the same period, UK imports from EU member states increased from 21 per cent to 50 per cent of the total. By 1994 Germany had overtaken the USA as Britain's leading trade partner. Links with Canada and Australia have declined. In contrast with other member states, though, Britain has maintained strong trading ties with the USA and has increased trading links with Japan, thereby indicating a continued preference for global rather than strictly regional trading connections.

One area of marked comparative advantage for the British economy is its strong service sector. However, moves towards EU service-industry liberalisation – in financial services and airlines, for example – have been slow. One major advantage for the British economy of the single market has therefore not yet been properly attained.

The key economic issue is, of course, EMU with its entangled political implications discussed in Chapter 5. Pro- and anti- EMU pressure groups are beginning to coalesce as battle lines are drawn for a referendum on the issue. At the Cardiff summit in June 1998 Prime Minister Blair uttered warm words about EMU: 'A single market with a single currency can bring enormous benefits. The euro will generate stability. It is in our interests that it succeeds.' This provoked a furious reaction from the *Sun* newspaper, which asked whether Blair was the most dangerous man in Britain. The Labour government appeared to be shifting the terms of debate towards economic issues and away from questions of national sovereignty. It is likely that a referendum on EMU in the UK will generate heated discussion of the euro's implications for national sovereignty.

A January 1999 ICM opinion poll for the *Guardian* newspaper found that opposition to EMU had increased in Britain at just the time that 11 other member states were embarking on the transition to a single currency. When asked if there was a referendum, whether they would vote to join the European single currency, 29 per cent of respondents said they would vote yes, 52 per cent that they would vote no, while 19 per cent were undecided. This compared to 34 per cent who said they would vote yes and 48 per cent who said they would vote no when the same question was asked in May 1998. Opposition to the euro was found to be stronger among working-class voters compared to middle-class voters. Readers of the *Sun*, *Daily Telegraph* and *Daily Mail* (all very hostile to the EU) were found to be particularly anti-euro.

Constitutional implications

The fundamental principle of Britain's unwritten constitution is parliamentary sovereignty. It has two main elements. Firstly, statute law passed by Parliament overrides other sources of law. Second, the principle of *lex posterior derogat priori* (later law overrides earlier) means that no Parliament can bind its successor. This has been compromised by membership of the EU because in areas where EU law has direct effect Parliament is no longer sovereign.

In its 1971 White Paper on the effects of membership the Heath government contended that, 'There is no question of any erosion of essential national sovereignty'. The key word here was 'essential'. A Labour MP begged to differ in the January 1972 debate on accession, and carried into the House of Commons 42 volumes containing 2500 EU regulations which would automatically become British law once Britain acceded to the Treaty of Rome.

In 1964 the ECJ had established the principle that EU law overrides national law (in the case of Costa vs ENEL). Thus, by joining Britain became subject to two apparently contradictory principles: statute law passed by the supposedly sovereign British Parliament that can be over-ridden by European law. The judiciary resolved this problem by treating European law as rules of construction. Cases of conflict between EU and national law would then be assumed to be a consequence of parliamentary error as the legislature was not likely to seek to contravene supranational obligations which it had itself assumed.

Scrutiny and accountability

The British Parliament has had difficulty scrutinising EU legislation and holding governments to account for their activities at Union level. The 'democratic deficit' which exists supranationally is thereby compounded by weak democratic control at the national level.

A series of mechanisms has been created to secure accountability. The prime minister reports on meetings of the European Council to the House of Commons, and the report is then debated. Questions on EU policy can be addressed to the prime minister or departmental ministers during parliamentary questions. A Select Committee on European Legislation with 16 members reports its opinion on the legal and political importance of EU legislation. It then recommends whether or not the legislation should be given further consideration in one of the European standing committees. There are two European Standing Committees in the House of Commons. Standing Committee 'A' considers agriculture, fisheries, food, forestry, the environment and transport. Committee 'B' considers all other documents. Each committee has 13 members, but any member of the House may attend and speak. Only members of the committee can vote on motions and proposed amendments. When a committee has reported then a motion relating to the documents is taken on the floor of the House of Commons without further debate, although amendments may be suggested. Other select committees can investigate Union matters that fall within their remit. The House of Lords has a committee on the EU which publishes detailed reports on Union activities. These have acquired a reputation for authority.

Despite this array of mechanisms, accountability is held to be lax. The House of Commons in particular needs to improve its scrutiny powers. It is currently deficient both in contributing to the development of EU policy, and in reviewing the progress of agreed policy. One problem is the sheer volume of proposals and legislation emanating from Brussels which must be considered alongside the existing workload of an already stretched legislature. It has been argued that national parliaments should work alongside the European Parliament in building effective scrutiny of EU decision-makers. There has, though, been little evidence of any concerted strategic vision that is likely to bring national parliaments into closer contact with the European Parliament.

Changing patterns of government

The EU has increasingly impinged on the actions of British government. The operation of the British state is heavily influenced by Union membership in a number of policy sectors. The initial point of contact between the EU and the British government is frequently the UK's permanent representation in Brussels (UKREP). UKREP services the work of the Council of Ministers through COREPER and can be very influential in the decision-making process. Some departments of state, such as the Foreign and Commonwealth Office and Trade, have been in touch with the Community since its inception in 1951. For others, particularly the Ministry of Agriculture, Fisheries and Food (MAFF), membership of the Union has meant a fundamental reorientation of their activities as what were once national policies are now common policies determined at the supranational level. As EU competence grows, Union membership is becoming an issue of increased salience for a range of government departments, such as the Home Office, Education and Environment. Even for interior ministries with responsibilities which have traditionally rendered them essentially national in orientation, there has been a development of a culture of cooperation on internal security issues linked to the single market.

The impact on local government has also been significant, but the absence of a regional tier of government means that the UK is not so well placed to benefit from a 'Europe of the regions' as are other member states. For the previous Conservative government, the principle of subsidiarity was seen as implying a shift towards national governments. The Blair Labour government has established subnational assemblies in Scotland, Wales and Northern Ireland which will have direct relations with the EU. If Labour were to secure a second term it is likely that regional government for England would be on the political agenda.

The Conservatives and Europe

A principal reason for the massive defeat suffered by the Conservative Party at the 1997 general election was divisions over Europe. These had bubbled to the surface in November 1990 when Thatcher was replaced by Major. Thatcher's forced resignation stemmed from her dispute with two leading cabinet ministers, Sir Geoffrey Howe and Nigel Lawson, over ERM membership. Howe wielded the dagger with a resignation speech that precipitated Michael Heseltine's leadership challenge and John Major's victory in the leadership contest.

The Maastricht deal secured by Major in December 1992 papered over the cracks in his party but the majority of 21 secured at the

1992 election meant that room for manoeuvre was limited in the face of even a relatively small number of backbenchers determined to do all they could to resist ratification of the Maastricht Treaty. The Danish 'No' in a June 1992 referendum on Maastricht emboldened the Eurosceptics, and more than 100 Conservative backbenchers called for a 'fresh start' and renegotiation. For a sizeable number of Tory backbenchers, Maastricht was a treaty too far. Only the resort to the 'nuclear option' of a confidence motion in the government allowed Maastricht's ratification. However, this did not calm dissent and Major felt he had no option but to resign the party leadership and invite challengers in June 1995. His victory over the former Welsh Secretary John Redwood was not entirely convincing.

One effect of opposition to further European integration on the Conservative backbenches was a determination not to be bound by a 1997 general election manifesto that failed to rule out a single currency. At the 1992 general election, Conservative candidates had stood on a manifesto that committed the party to Maastricht ratification. The party's whips reminded them of this fact during the ratification process. From the summer of 1996, Eurosceptic MPs began to canvas the adoption of a common line to be taken in the personal manifestos of Eurosceptic MPs and candidates in opposition to the single currency. A millionaire businessman offered donations to Conservative candidates prepared to rule out a single currency. By 30 April 1997, 237 candidates in Conservative-held seats had accepted donations. The party's manifesto committed candidates to a 'wait and see' policy. Many of the candidates were patently not prepared to support this position. Even ministers in the previous Conservative government ruled out support for a single currency. Major was unable to sack them for this dissent because to do so would be to risk re-opening old wounds.

Major was caught between a rising tide of Euroscepticism within his party and a small number of Europhiles who made up in influence for what they lacked in numbers. Major's two most senior cabinet ministers, Chancellor of the Exchequer Kenneth Clarke and Deputy Prime Minister Michael Heseltine, were firmly pro-European. Survey evidence from an analysis of Conservative Party members conducted in 1992 pointed to Euroscepticism within the party, but also noted that between one fifth and one third of party members were staunch pro-Europeans.

When elected as party leader in the summer of 1997, William Hague ruled out Conservative participation in a single currency for 10 years. This made the Conservatives the anti-EMU party, although leading backbenchers such as Clarke, Heseltine and former cabinet minister Stephen Dorrell adopt a distinctly more pro-European line. An analysis of Conservative MPs conducted after the 1997 general election revealed a tilt in the direction of Euroscepticism: 21 per cent of Conservative MPs were classified as being on the pro-integration left-wing of the party, with 30 per cent on the anti-integration right wing. The rest were classed as party loyalists, but of these 34 per cent had sceptical leanings. The sceptics clearly held the upper hand, but the presence of a sizeable number of Europhiles, including some of the party's biggest names, suggest that the issue is far from resolved.

Labour and Europe

Neither of the two main parties has been consistent in its European policies. In the late 1970s and early 1980s, the Conservatives were the more pro-European of the two main parties. In 1983 Labour's manifesto claimed that 'withdrawal from the Community is the right policy for Britain'. By 1997 the party promised a more constructive engagement than the Conservatives had been able to deliver. But, like many other issues at the 1997 general election, Labour exhibited some caution which meant that on the key policy issues there was actually little to choose between the main parties.

Labour's 1997 general election manifesto called for 'an alliance of independent nations choosing to co-operate to achieve the goals they cannot achieve alone. We oppose a federal European superstate.' This language did not differ markedly from that in the Conservative manifesto. On the euro, both Labour and the Conservatives pledged to hold a referendum to reach a decision on membership. Labour also pledged to uphold the national veto on taxation, defence and security, immigration, the budget and treaty changes. The main difference between the two parties was in their stance on the Social Chapter. Labour pledged to sign up, although as has been seen, it brought to government a commitment to labour market and welfare state changes that indicate an aversion to increased EU social policy regulation: 'flexibility' is the watchword.

The new Labour government held the EU presidency for the first six months of 1998 during which time the European Conference brought together current and future EU member states. A decision was also reached on participants in the single currency and a rather messy compromise was secured for the appointment of the first president of the European Central Bank. The Labour government faced a difficult balancing act on the euro. As Council president it was obliged to push forward the process while making it clear that it would not participate in the first wave of third-stage members. There was also the issue of public hostility to the euro. In October 1997, 29 per cent of British people surveyed in a Eurobarometer opinion poll supported participation in the euro, 59 per cent were opposed. According to this poll, Britain was the most hostile country to the euro. Sections of the national press have also maintained a strong anti-euro line. The *Sun*'s picture of Blair on its front cover and question as to whether he was the most dangerous man in Britain was only the most extreme manifestation of a deep hostility in some sections of the British press to European integration.

Tony Blair's first ministerial reshuffle was seen as consolidating a pro-European axis within the government. Peter Mandelson became Secretary of State for Trade and Industry to form a powerful pro-euro coalition with Chancellor Gordon Brown. However, tensions dating back to the election of Blair as Labour Party leader resurfaced in December 1998, with the result that Mandelson resigned following revelations of a 'soft loan' from a fellow government minister, Geoffrey Robinson. In the summer reshuffle, the businessman David Sainsbury joined the Department of Trade and Industry in an unpaid role which the *Guardian* noted 'amounts to an extra pair of hands which might be used to drive the single-currency campaign among businessmen'.[1]

Attitudes of other parties

Within Britain the Liberal Democrats have been the most consistently European party. In their previous incarnation as the Liberal Party they urged membership of the ECSC in 1951 and of the EEC and Euratom in 1957. Furthermore, it was the anti-EU stance of the left-dominated Labour Party that prompted creation of the SDP and an eventual realignment of centre-party politics in Britain. In their 1997 general election manifesto the Liberal Democrats maintained their consistent line on European integration, calling for a 'decentralised, democratic and diverse' federal Europe. In July 1998, the Liberal Democrat leader, Paddy Ashdown, called for a written constitution for the EU to match the powerful economic arrangements being established for the euro. He argued that EMU would create 'an immensely powerful economic institution, set within an immensely weak and shambolic political one. This will very quickly prove unsustainable. We will be forced by events, if not by our own people, to strengthen our political institutions so as to contain and counter-balance it'.

The Scottish National Party (SNP) opposed membership of the EU until 1983. During the 1980s its attitude softened to the point at which, in 1988, it endorsed the EU under the slogan 'Scotland within

Europe'. The SNP recognised that fear of isolation was a factor contributing to lack of support for independence and that anchoring Scotland to a federal Europe could allay it. It also realised the importance of Brussels as a source of aid for the Scottish economy, which has been hit hard by the decline in manufacturing industry. The SNP is also keen to develop links with other regionalist parties in Europe.

In Wales Plaid Cymru seeks a self-governing Wales in the EU. Plaid Cymru has been increasingly influenced by green political thinking which in its 1997 general election manifesto led to an emphasis on sustainability and reform of the CAP embodying agri-environmental objectives. Plaid also called for ambitious institutional reforms with a bicameral European parliamentary system, with a second chamber (senate) representing the nations and regions of the EU; a confederal written constitution, and a bill of rights for Europe. In time, Plaid wished to see the power of the Council of Ministers transferred to the European Parliament and Senate, which would be solely responsible for making law.

The Green Party in 1989 took 14.9 per cent of the vote in European Parliament elections, but gained no seats. The Greens favour continued membership of the EU while seeking reform from within. They oppose continued British membership if the EU is not reconstituted on sound ecological principles.

In Northern Ireland both the Ulster Unionists (UUP) and the Democratic Unionists (DUP) oppose membership of the Community, although each takes seats in the European Parliament to lobby its part of Ulster's population. Northern Ireland has received more development aid than any other part of the UK (£940 million between 1994 and 1999). Unionists fear that European integration may erode the border between Northern Ireland and the Republic of Ireland. These suspicions were heightened when a 1984 European Parliament report called for more power sharing. DUP leader, the Reverend Ian Paisley, has used his Strasbourg seat to denounce the Papist conspiracy that he sees as central to the Community. The nationalist Social Democratic and Labour Party (SDLP) endorses membership and has advocated an EU role in solving the Northern Ireland problem. The SDLP's leader, John Hume, has said that EU membership provides a 'new and positive context for the discussion of sovereignty'. The political wing of the Provisional IRA, Sinn Fein, is opposed to membership of the capitalist EU.[2]

At the 1997 general election two explicitly anti-EU parties fielded candidates. The Referendum Party was lavishly funded by the billionaire financier Sir James Goldsmith. It called for a referendum on Britain's future relations with Europe and explicitly rejected federalism. The party attracted immense publicity but relatively few votes. It contested 547 seats and garnered 810,778 votes, which, when the £20 million spent by Goldsmith on the party is taken into account, works out at nearly £25 a vote. The UK Independence Party (UKIP) was overshadowed by Goldsmith's dramatic entry on to the British political scene. The UKIP was committed to withdrawal from the EU which it claimed would save £19 billion a year.

Pressure groups and the EU

Pressure groups go where power goes: as power in a number of key sectors has gone to the Union level, so pressure groups have re-focused their activities on the EU. This re-focusing is supposed to be an important part of the neo-functionalist integrative dynamic.

The first step for a national pressure group seeking to lobby at the supranational level is to find an analogous 'Eurogroup', of which there are more than 500. Due to its small size and consequent lack of resources (time, money, expertise and so on), the Commission is extremely attentive to pressure groups. Within the EU policy process industrial and agricultural groups have tended to dominate.[3]

In Britain the Confederation of British Industry (CBI) has been consistently pro-EU since the 1960s. It has its own Brussels office in the building which houses its EU analogue UNICE (a French acronym for the Union of Industries of the EC). In recent years the CBI has helped harden UNICE attitudes on Community social policies. It supported the Conservative government's opt-out from the Social Chapter. It has expressed some reservations about the two directives introduced under the Social Chapter – the Works Council and Parental Leave directives – because it holds that the EU should avoid what it sees as the mistaken labour-market policies pursued in some member states.

During the period of Conservative government the Trades Union Congress (TUC) appeared to view EU responsibility for economic and social cohesion as a beacon of hope for a beleaguered labour movement. This was despite the fact that the trade unions spent most of the 1970s and 1980s opposing British membership. The turning point was Labour's electoral defeat in 1983, which prompted new 'realist' leaders, such as Bill Jordan of the Amalgamated Union of Engineering Workers, to argue that trade unionists needed to make the Community work for them in the same way that industry had. The TUC's reorientation was confirmed by the wave of Euroenthusiasm which swept through its 1988 conference, when Commission President Jacques Delors received a standing ovation for his speech on the benefits of EU membership for the labour movement.[4] The utilisation of European opportunities is a key part of the TUC's partnership with government and industry that forms part of the 'New Deal' at the heart of the Blair government's 'welfare to work' strategy.

Public opinion

Opinion poll evidence suggests that the EU is a low salience issue in the minds of most British people, lagging far behind (un)employment, education, management of the economy and other day-to-day concerns. Until 1990-91 there was a steady growth in the number of British people who were either very much or to some extent in favour of European unification. The level of 71 per cent registered in 1990 compares with 63 per cent in 1980. Since 1990 Euroscepticism has set in. Opinion polls suggest Britons to be among the least enthusiastic Europeans. To what extent this was prompted by a Conservative government that was wracked by internal division and at times overtly hostile to European integration may become clearer if and when the influence on public opinion of a more pro-European Labour government becomes detectable.

In an October 1997 opinion poll 36 per cent of UK respondents said that EU membership was a good thing, compared to 23 per cent who said it was a bad thing. This was a significant drop in support since 1990, when more than 70 per cent had said it was a good thing. In 1997 37 per cent of respondents thought that the UK had benefited from EU membership, but 43 per cent thought it had not. For the EU as a whole, 44 per cent of respondents in the 15 member states thought that their country had benefited, compared with 35 per cent who thought it had not. Across the EU, this marked a drop in support and perceptions of the benefits of European integration. This has been linked with economic recession because support for European integration tends to dwindle in such times. There may, though, be more to it than that. The Maastricht ratification process did reveal unease in a number of member states, reflected in longer than planned ratification processes about the pace of European integration and a perceived gap between political elites and the people of Europe.

Opinion polls also suggest that even though there was a steady increase in UK support for European integration during the 1980s there has been a decline since 1990. Favourable publicity associated with the single market, which was portrayed in extremely positive terms, may have accounted for much of this increase, but is there still a gap between perceptions in the UK and in other member states? People in the UK tend to be less enthusiastic about European integration than people in other member states. There is also a difference between affective and utilitarian support for the Community.[5] In Britain affective loyalty to the aspiration of European unity exceeds that of utilitarian support for the current form of unification (the EU). Support dwindled after 1991 when the Maastricht Treaty and the civil war in the Conservative Party led to a largely negative portrayal of European integration. In Britain opposition to the euro is most prevalent.

How deep these sentiments run is another important issue because opinion-poll evidence also suggests a lack of knowledge about the EU. In October 1997 people were asked to locate themselves on a 10-point scale ranging from 'know nothing at all about the EU' to 'know a great deal'. The UK ranked fourteenth out of 15 on this measure with a score of 3.38. Austrians were at the top of the scale with 4.81, but even they hardly displayed an avid interest in all things European. In such circumstances opinion may be more malleable and prone to change because views are not so firmly cast.

A reluctant European?

If we were to use opinion poll evidence as our guide, then the British people would seem to be reluctant Europeans. British governments have also adopted an at times ambivalent and at other times hostile stance towards European integration. No British government has adopted a strong pro-European position. The Labour government elected in 1997 has emphasised its pro-Europeanness, but this has yet to be tested by major European problems. How much this reluctance is to do with negative coverage of European issues and the attitudes of successive governments, and how much it is associated with a deeper and longer-standing ambivalence to economic and political integration is uncertain. It is clear that when European issues became controversial in British politics after 1990, and hostility among politicians and from the media grew, anti-EU sentiment also grew in strength.

Reluctance must be placed alongside an increased 'Europeanisation' of British economics and politics which can be seen in the changed activities of central government, local authorities, political parties and pressure groups. If this is suggestive of a disjunction between political elites and the British people then it is possible to speculate that there is an opportunity for a political party to exploit anti-European sentiment. It seems that the Conservatives are positioning themselves as the most sceptical of the main parties. The dangers of this strategy are two-fold. Firstly, a tough line on the EU could reopen splits in the party. Second, European integration is not a salient concern for many voters. A party that develops an anti-EU platform may be seen to neglect concerns such as the economy and welfare that are more important in voters' minds.

In terms of sovereignty arguments, it seems that Britain's tradition comprises an 'expansive' rather than a 'pooled' sovereignty, and that the British have found it particularly hard to come to terms with their changed status in the world. Many argue that Britain's greatness is in the past, and that the challenge of the modern era is to respond to patterns of interdependence that increasingly link Britain to the EU. However, historical and political analysis cannot be reduced to a series of trade (or other) statistics. A range of factors tempers British enthusiasm for European integration and generates British reluctance.

Notes

1 M. White, 'Pro-Europeans move up as Blair ends reshuffle', *Guardian*, 29 July 1998, p3.

2 J Tonge, *Northern Ireland: Conflict and Change* (Prentice Hall, Hemel Hempstead, 1998).

3 S Mazey and J Richardson, *Lobbying in the European Community* (Oxford University Press, Oxford, 1993).

4 Trades Union Congress, Europe 1992: Maximising the Benefits, Minimising the Costs (TUC, London, 1988).

5 M Hewstone, *Understanding Attitudes to the European Community: A Socio-Psychological Study in Four Member States* (Cambridge University Press, Cambridge, 1986).

Conclusion

European integration raises fundamental questions that stir strong opinions. In Britain, these debates are refracted through an historical and social context that leads to particular perspectives being taken on key issues such as the relationship between supranationalism and national sovereignty. Many Eurosceptics evince a strong notion of national sovereignty and emphasise Britain's global rather than European connections. Europhiles contend that such views hark back to the past and that Britain is now inextricably linked with the EU and should become a wholehearted participant.

Debates about sovereignty have a particular British context reflecting Britain's history and self-image. Perceptions of national sovereignty and its merits do, however, mean different things in other member states. As evidence for this a core group of member states has been determined to push towards closer economic and political integration. Britain has in the past underestimated this determination or thought it to be unrealistic. Yet evidence suggests that this drive towards some kind of federal Europe remains.

This drive for deeper integration does face huge challenges in the first decade of the twenty-first century, when it is likely that a currency union will be established and membership will increase to more than 20 member states. These developments raise important questions for the EU to which the British government must also respond. Can an EU with more than 20 member states be a more politically and economically integrated EU? Is the future of Europe likely to be one of greater 'flexibility' where some states move more quickly to achieve integrative objectives while others lag behind? If this happens, will Britain eschew closer cooperation and prefer to be at the outer core of the EU? On the basis of its opt-outs on the euro and free movement of people, Britain seems to prefer the outer core. But if it does then how can it hope to do what its leaders often claim they want to do: take a leading position in the EU?

A wider and deeper Europe   It is fairly usual for a new British prime minister to claim that he or she wants to establish a more constructive relationship with the EU. Tony Blair was not unique when he made such comments in May 1997. But the challenges presented by European integration raise fundamental questions about Britain's ability to shape events and move from being a constructive partner to a country that exercises a leading role. This is for two main reasons. Firstly, as membership expands in central, eastern and southern Europe, the geographical axis of the Union will tilt eastwards. Germany's position at the heart of Europe will be reinforced and the Franco-German relationship is likely to remain the EU's foundation stone. Second, if as seems very likely a currency union is successfully established then the UK will not participate. Britain will watch from the sidelines as integration occurs from which it is voluntarily excluded and the development of which it has been unable decisively to influence. The EU is likely to be both wider and deeper, but neither of these developments seems to offer the possibility of a more central role for Britain.

If Britain is to have an impact on EU developments then this may derive from attempts to translate a domestic policy agenda to the EU level. Modernisation of the UK has a European dimension, the British government has argued. The EU, it is thought, could learn useful lessons from Labour's pursuit of what is called the 'third way' between free-market capitalism and socialism. Although this is not the most precisely defined political programme, it has formed the basis for attempts to forge links with centre-left parties in other member states. Meanwhile, Labour's emphasis on labour-market flexibility and 'welfare-to-work' tie in with euro-induced changes in labour markets and welfare-state arrangements in other EU member states. But while Britain remains outside the euro real influence is likely to be more difficult to wield. On the most basic issue, there is little evidence that the British people are warming to the prospect of the euro replacing the pound.

Flexible Europe

The tension between those member states which adopt a more max-imalist position on European integration and those such as Britain which have favoured a more minimalist approach underpins the Amsterdam Treaty's provisions for closer cooperation, or flexibility as it is also known. This means that maximalist countries have the opportunity to integrate more rapidly without being held back either by more reluctant member states or by those unable to make the transition to deeper integration. Flexibility takes into account the important political ambitions that underpin the EU, and which has made it far more than just a free-trade arrangement.

Eleven member states pushed towards the third stage of EMU that was attained on 1 January 1999. Meanwhile, 12 member states are committed to the establishment of free movement and the develop-ment of common immigration and asylum policies within a five-year period after ratification of the Amsterdam Treaty. This flexibility scenario has at its core a centripetal integrative impetus which acknowledges the formidable 'logic' that underpins integration and is closely linked to the aspirations of core member states. It guarantees, of course, neither the success nor the desirability of the federal goals which remain intensely controversial issues in the UK and other EU member states. An important point, however, is that these debates in Britain often reveal as much, if not more, about Britain, than they do about the EU. Much of the recent discussion about European integration in British politics is linked to a rather longer-standing debate about Britain's self-perception and role in world affairs. Meanwhile the EU bandwagon rolls on.

Britain in the slow lane?

It seems that despite protestations of a desire to be constructive, Britain has a marginal relation to central aspects of European integration. Moreover, marginality is to a considerable extent self-imposed. It is hard to envisage Britain being at the heart of a flexible Europe. Indeed, current policy stances on the euro and free movement indicate a preference for the outer core, with no hard and fast commitment to eventual participation.

Indeed, during the 1990s the tenor of debate about European integration has changed quite markedly. Euroscepticism has become a more powerful force in British politics than it had been since the mid-1970s. In the early 1990s it had seemed fairly safe to say that the debate about membership had been resolved: Britain was for better or worse an EC member state. Opponents of membership found it difficult to put forward a credible alternative. To some extent this changed during the 1990s. It is still the case that a powerful political coalition backed by key economic interests and stretching across the main political parties favours participation. This coalition accepts with greater or lesser enthusiasm what is seen as Britain's European destiny. In some quarters, however, opinion has hardened, and even in the two main political parties there are those who have mooted, for instance, some kind of withdrawal from the EU with a renegotiated trading relationship *à la* Norway. These opinions are hardly in the political mainstream, but in 1997 they did find some resonance in the activities of the Referendum Party and the UK Independence Party. These parties, notably the former, were better at getting publicity than at getting votes, but they did draw hostility to the EU closer to mainstream political debate.

While economic and political integration move to deeper levels Britain's stance remains ambivalent. The government is constrained in its scope for action by a sceptical public hardened in its attitude to

European integration by seven or eight years of almost unremittingly negative coverage. The EU has a credibility problem. People have little interest in it and what little they do know about it often tends not to lead to a positive evaluation. For Prime Minister Blair to turn aspiration into reality and develop a leading EU role for Britain, there is a need firstly to convince other member states that Britain's commitment to integration is serious, and second, to convince the British people that European integration offers real benefits.

It seems that rather long-standing problems are central to an evaluation of Britain's role in the EU. When rejecting Britain's first application for membership in 1963 General de Gaulle stated that: 'Great Britain is moving towards Europe, but it has not yet arrived.' Thirty-five years later, and after more than 25 years of membership, this statement is still apposite. Although Britain is substantially Europeanised, many British people and many of their leaders remain reluctant or cautious Europeans.

Appendix

1948	March	Brussels Treaty establishes a collective defence organisation comprising France, Britain and the Benelux countries
	April	Organisation for European Economic Cooperation (OEEC) established with 16 member states
	May	Congress of Europe meets in The Hague
1949	April	Treaty of Washington signed by 12 member states establishes NATO
	May	Council of Europe established
1950	May	French foreign minister Robert Schuman puts forward plan for a coal and steel community
1951	April	Treaty of Paris establishes the European Coal and Steel Community (ECSC) with six members (France, West Germany, Italy and the Benelux countries)
1954	August	French National Assembly rejects plans for a European Defence Community (EDC). West European Union (WEU) established as an intergovernmental collective defence organisation
1955	June	Messina conference of ECSC foreign ministers discusses further integration
1957	March	Treaties of Rome establish the European Economic Community (EEC) and Euratom with six founder members (France, West Germany, Italy and the Benelux countries)
1959	July	Stockholm Convention establishes the European Free Trade Area (EFTA) with seven members (Austria, Britain, Denmark, Norway, Portugal, Sweden and Switzerland)
1963	January	General de Gaulle vetoes Britain's first application for EU membership
1965	July	France begins a boycott of Community institutions in protest at supranational developments

1966	January	Luxembourg Accord agrees use of national vetoes and allows normal Community decision-making procedures to resume
1968	July	EEC Customs Union established, with the result that all internal duties and quotas are removed and the Common External Tariff is put in place for goods from outside the Community
1969	July	Georges Pompidou announces that he does not oppose British membership
1970	April	Community budgetary process established
1972	January	Britain, Denmark, Ireland and Norway sign Treaties of Accession to the EC
	September	Norwegian people vote 'No' to Community membership
1973	January	Accession of Britain, Denmark and Ireland
1975	June	Referendum on British membership of the Community produces a two to one vote in favour of continued participation
1979	June	First direct elections to the European Parliament
1981	January	Accession of Greece
1984	June	Second set of direct elections to the European Parliament. Fontainebleau summit produces a budget rebate for Britain
1985	June	Commission publishes its White Paper, Completing the Internal Market
1986	January	Accession of Spain and Portugal
	June	Single European Act (SEA) establishes plan for completion of the single market by the end of 1992
1988	February	Brussels European Council meeting agrees a five-year financial perspective for the Community which raises the budget from 1.14 per cent of member states' GNP to 1.20 per cent
1989	April	Delors Report presents a three-stage plan for EMU
	June	Third set of direct elections to the European Parliament

1989	September	Soviet bloc crumbles, beginning with the appointment of a non-Communist Prime Minister in Poland and ending with the overthrow of Ceaucescu in Romania
	December	Strasbourg European Council meeting adopts the Social Charter and agrees to convene an intergovernmental conference on economic and monetary union (EMU). Both decisions are taken by 11 votes to one, with Britain the dissenter
1990	October	Reunification of Germany leads to incorporation of the former GDR in the Community
	December	Intergovernmental conferences on economic and political union opened at the Rome European Council
1991	December	Maastricht Summit agrees the Treaty on European Union which, among other things, gives the three-stage plan for EMU legal effect
1992	June	The Danes vote 'No' to Maastricht by 51 per cent to 49 per cent
	September	Sterling forced out of the ERM The French referendum returns a 'petit oui' to Maastricht by 51 per cent to 49 per cent
	December	Edinburgh European Council meeting agrees a financial perspective to take the Community through to the end of the century, by which time the Community budget will amount to 1.27 per cent of member states' GNP
1993	August	Heavy speculative pressure on the ERM leads to a widening of its bands to 15 per cent Britain ratifies the Maastricht Treaty
1994	June	Fourth set of direct elections to the European Parliament
	December	Corfu summit convenes IGC
1995	January	Accession of Austria, Finland and Sweden
1997	June	Amsterdam Treaty negotiated
	July	Commission presents Agenda 2000 programme
1998	March	First European Conference brings together current and prospective EU member states
	May	Participants in third stage of EMU announced

1999	January	Stage Three of EMU commences with 11 participating states
	March	Special European Council to discuss Agenda 2000

A brief guide to further reading

There are many good books on the EU. More recently, the internet has become an excellent source for up-to-date information.

For an historical overview of European integration, see D Urwin, *The Community of Europe* (Longman, London, 1991). For detailed analysis of specific events in Community history, see R Pryce (ed) *The Dynamics of European Union* (Croom Helm, London, 1987). J Story (ed), *The New Europe* (Blackwell, Oxford, 1993), assesses the impact on the Community of major events in the 1980s and early 1990s (such as the end of the Cold War and plans for EMU). For a good account of the various European organisations that have emerged in the post-war era, see C Archer, *Organizing Western Europe*, second edition (Edward Arnold, London, 1994). Also see J Lodge, *Integration and Cooperation in Europe* (Routledge, London, 1992).

The best book on EU institutions is N Nugent, *The Government and Politics of the European Union*, third edition (Macmillan, London, 1994). On Community policies see D Swann, *The Economics of the Common Market*, eighth edition (Penguin, Harmondsworth, 1995), and L Tsoukalis, *The New European Economy Revisited*, third edition (Oxford University Press, Oxford, 1997).

On Britain and the EU, S George, *An Awkward Partner: Britain in the European Community*, third edition (Oxford University Press, Oxford, 1998), gives a good overview of British government policies. S Greenwood, *Britain and European Cooperation since 1945* (Blackwell, Oxford, 1992), looks more closely at events prior to accession.

Academic journals are good sources of up-to-date information on developments in the EU. Many journals contain articles relating to the EU, though two are particularly valuable. The *Journal of Common Market Studies* and the *Journal of European Public Policy* focus on the EU. The *Journal of Common Market Studies* also carries an annual review of EU activities. *International Affairs* has a strong focus on events in Europe.

For those seeking more detailed information, a number of academic libraries contain European Documentation Centres within which a large amount of the EU's own documents can be found.

There is also a vast amount of information on EU activities on the internet. Good starting points for eager surfers are the EU's own home page: <http://europa.eu.int> and a collection of EU resources gathered at: <http://fgr.wu-wien.ac.at/nentwich/euroint.htm>.

Index